D1563145

BIRTH CONTROL
AND THE
MARRIAGE COVENANT

JOHN F. KIPPLEY

Birth Control
and the
Marriage Covenant

THE LITURGICAL PRESS

Collegeville, Minnesota

Nihil Obstat: Daniel V. Flynn, J.C.D., Censor Librorum. Imprimatur:
† Joseph O'Brien, S.T.D., V.G., Archdiocese of New York. May 2, 1970.
LC: 79-129174; ISBN 0-8146-0915-5. Copyright © 1976 by The Order
of St. Benedict, Inc., Collegeville, MN 56321. Printed and bound in the
U.S.A.

PREFACE TO THE SECOND EDITION

In the six years since the first edition of this book[1], the doctrine of marital non-contraception, reaffirmed in 1968 by *Humanae Vitae*, has continued to be a point of controversy. Perhaps this will continue for the indefinite future, but I should not be at all surprised to see a growing acceptance of this traditional Christian belief between the eighth and fifteenth anniversaries of that encyclical. There are several reasons for saying this.

1. For one thing, the theologizing that has sought to justify and promote dissent has simply failed to justify its own position, and its logical consequences cannot be evaded for long. For example, at the same time this book was first published, a book promoting dissent also appeared.[2] Its author very clearly spelled out the logic of the dissenters. (He called them revisionists and included himself among them.) According to him, the revisionists in their rejection of the tradition of marital non-contraception had rejected the entire natural law theory used to support it; therefore, they could not argue against any sexual behavior between consenting adults — or even bestiality — on the grounds that such behavior was contrary to the very nature

---

1. First published under the title *Covenant, Christ and Contraception*. New York: Alba House, 1970.
2. Michael Valenti. *Sex: The Radical View of A Catholic Theologian.* New York: Bruce, 1970.

of mankind. These conclusions in all their bluntness have not been welcomed by the more popular theologians of dissent who have apparently preferred either 1) not to think through their dissent to the logical conclusions or 2) not to share these conclusions with the general public which isn't yet conditioned to accept them. Nevertheless, the inner logic cannot be denied, and these logical consequences will gradually come to the fore. It is my hope that once such practical conclusions are out in the open, the great majority of Christians will recognize that such practices are totally incompatible with Christian discipleship and will then recognize the error of the starting point: the rejection of the teaching of *Humanae Vitae*.

To cite another example, a recognized leader of dissent, Father Charles Curran, has said that he would "re-think" his position on extra-marital sex (as of early 1976, he still frowned on it) if a number of married couples told him that they found it helpful for their overall marriage. To those who have followed the theology of Fr. Curran, such "re-thinking" means that he would provide some sort of personalistic basis for "justifying" adultery, at least where it was by mutual consent. Is this acknowledged leader of dissent believable as an interpreter of Christian morality? If he is not believable when it comes to wife-swapping, why should he be believable if he uses the same principles to justify marital contraception?

In an effort to analyze the principles behind the dissent from *Humanae Vitae,* I have written two articles that appeared in *Theological Studies* (March, 1971) and the *Linacre Quarterly* (February, 1974). The first criticized the principles of dissent and moral decision making as enunciated by Charles Curran. The second provided a critical analysis of several dissent positions, including the application of the principle of proportionality to the marriage act. To the best of my knowledge, neither article has been criticized as being unfair or inaccurate. Both of these articles have been included as appendices in the present edition.

2. Another reason for believing that there will be an increasing belief in the Christian tradition of marital non-contra-

ception is that the middle 1970's have witnessed a growing disenchantment with the Pill and the IUD on the purely pragmatic grounds of medical side effects. (At the moral level, some reject these because the IUD is primarily an abortion-causing device and the Pill may also act as such at any given time.) Simultaneously, there has been an increasing interest in the natural-methods-only approach to birth regulation, and there has likewise been an increasing availability of information both in the form of written materials and practical instructions. Reference to some of these is provided in Appendix I in this edition.

3. A third reason for believing that the steam has about run out of the dissent movement is that after several years of relative silence, bishops are once again beginning to reaffirm *Humanae Vitae* with clarity and vigor. In this vein, one of the most helpful signs is the 1973 statement of the Canadian bishops. In 1968, that episcopal conference issued a post-*Humanae Vitae* statement that was widely interpreted to mean "If you don't agree with the Pope, don't let your practice of contraception bother your conscience," — regardless of the precise wording of their statement. However, in 1973, their statement was open to no such interpretation:

"...If his ultimate practical judgment to do this or avoid that does not take into full account the teaching of the Church, an account based not only on reason but on the faith dimension, he is deceiving himself in pretending that he is acting as a true Catholic must. For a Catholic, 'to follow one's conscience' is not then, simply to act as his unguided reason dictates. 'To follow one's conscience' and to remain a Catholic, one must take into account first and foremost the teaching of the magisterium. When doubt arises due to a conflict of 'my' views and those of the magisterium, the presumption of truth lies on the part of the magisterium...." (Statement on the Formation of Conscience, paragraphs 40 and 41.)

My own experience indicates that this document is almost unknown among the clergy and laity of the United States; I would suggest that it would make an excellent subject for parish discussion groups.[3]

Thus, it is with a sense of Christian hope that I have written this preface to the second edition. I suppose we shall always have the die-hards who will never be able to question their own dissent, but I think that a growing number of people are willing to examine their past practice of recommending or using contraceptives and abortifacients in the light of the types of things mentioned above. Furthermore, I want to think that there are increasing numbers of people who want to live according to the Spirit, knowing full well that such a way of life involves the difficulty of sexual self-control; I want to think that increasing numbers of people desire to walk with Jesus on what He has told is the narrow way to eternal life. For these and others who are looking for a theological explanation of the Christian tradition of marital non-contraception, I hope that this book provides help; and to those who presently hold a position of dissent, I hope that this book offers a challenge.

May 5, 1976

". . . The fruit of the Spirit is love, joy, peace, patience, kindness, goodness, faithfulness, gentleness, self-control; against such there is no law. And those who belong to Christ Jesus have crucified the flesh with its passions and desires. If we live by the Spirit, let us also walk by the Spirit."

— Galatians 5:22-25.

---

3. Canadian Catholic Conference. *Statement on the Formation of Conscience.* Available in a 25c pamphlet from the Daughters of St. Paul, 50 St. Paul's Av., Jamaica Plain, Boston, Mass. 02130.

ACKNOWLEDGMENTS

Grateful acknowledgment is hereby made for permission to quote from the following published works:
The Belknap Press of Harvard University Press for permission to quote from *Contraception* by John T. Noonan, Jr. *Commonweal* for permission to quote from an article by Gregory Baum. Fides Publishers for permission to quote from *Christian Morality Today* by Charles Curran. The *Globe and Mail* of Toronto for permission to quote from an article by Gregory Baum. Helicon Press for permission to quote from *The Pill* by Leo Pyle © 1964 by Leo Pyle. Liverwright Publishing Corp. for permission to quote from *A General Introduction to Psycho-Analysis* by Sigmund Freud. The Macmillan Company for permission to quote from *The Secular City* by Harvey Cox © 1965 by Harvey Cox. The *National Catholic Reporter* for permission to quote from the documents contained in *The Birth Control Debate*. The Paulist-Newman Press for permission to quote from *Toward a Christian Ethic* by William Van Der Marck, O.P. © 1967 by the Missionary Society of St. Paul the Apostle. Sheed and Ward, New York, for permission to quote from *On Consulting the Faithful in Matters of Doctrine* by John Henry Newman, © Copyright, Introduction and edited text, 1961, John Coulson. Sheed and Ward, Ltd., London, for permission to quote from *Love and Fertility* by William Van Der Marck, O.P. *Theological Studies* for permission to quote from the issue of June, 1968. Biblical quotes are from the Revised Standard Version of the *Oxford Annotated Bible,* copyrighted in 1965 by the Oxford University Press, Inc. The author wishes to thank also the editors of *Ave Maria* for permission to use material already published therein.

TABLE OF CONTENTS

INTRODUCTION

THE STATED DOCTRINE

1. A Short Historical Resumé

In the debate that has ensued since the promulgation of *Humanae Vitae,* the question has been raised as to whether or not the Church really has anything to say about the whole question of contraception. The presently definitive work on the history of the doctrine of non-contraception has been written by John T. Noonan, Jr.[1] It is a masterful and diligent study of the treatment of the question over the centuries by Catholic theologians and the magisterium. The history is so extensive that any attempt to provide a resumé is bound to be inadequate. Nevertheless, it may be worthwhile to note a few points in passing.

First of all, the practice of contraception is nothing new to mankind. Records dating from 1900 B.C. show the contraceptive effort in the Mediterranean world of that time. There is every indication that it was an accepted practice in the Roman empire during the beginnings of the Christian era. I mention this because at the popular level I have heard arguments that only through modern science have we found contraception. The pop-

---

1. *Contraception: A History of Its Treatment by Catholic Theologians and Canonists* (Cambridge, Mass.: The Belknap Press of Harvard University Press, 1965).

ular argument sees in this almost a divine guidance of science, a new cure for a population problem that didn't exist previously. Noonan makes it quite clear that although modern science has greatly improved the technique, the practice of contraception is ancient.

Secondly, the question about contraceptive acts has been raised in a number of different ways over the centuries of the Christian era. Apparently the Gnostics in the first century were teaching an extreme doctrine which permitted intercourse for anyone provided that procreation was avoided. Marriage was either attacked or ignored as the stable means of continuing the human race. Sexual intercourse was seen both as the supreme good (and therefore mandatory for everyone regardless of marital status) or as an abominable evil in a dualistic system of spirit and matter. The Cathars of the Middle Ages condemned marriage and especially sexual relations in marriage as evil. However, they did not practice complete continence but had non-marital liaisons which they regarded as permissible. Procreation was seen as evil.

Thirdly, the response of the magisterium to these various doctrines has been constant in its emphasis that intercourse is moral only within marriage and that intercourse must remain open to procreation. It is fair to say that in various ways the question of contraception has been with us since the beginning of Christianity and that for nineteen centuries the Church has provided a constant answer forbidding contraception regardless of how the question was raised. For one who believes that the Church is led by the Holy Spirit, it is also quite believable that this constant teaching of the Church is the fruit of the Spirit. Such a belief does not say that our philosophizing and theologizing cannot be improved, but it does conclude that contraception is a moral evil.

2.   Pius XI: *Casti Connubii*

The Catholic tradition of non-contraception has always taken verbal form as a reaction to the philosophy and the practice of the age. The statement of Pius XI was no exception. Birth control had been the subject of conferences since the turn of the century. Margaret Sanger began her work, some national hierarchies issued statements, and questions of confessional policy with regard to contraception were frequently asked of Rome.

In 1930 matters reached a climax. In the June issue of *Hochland,* a German Catholic periodical, a call was issued for a change in the teaching on contraception. On August 15, the Lambeth Conference of Anglican bishops which had condemned contraception in both 1908 and 1920 broke its tradition and permitted contraception. On December 31, the reply of Pope Pius XI renewed in a formal way the tradition of the Catholic Church in his encyclical *Casti Connubii*:

> Assuredly no reason, even the most serious, can make congruent with nature and decent what is intrinsically against nature. Since the act of the spouses is by its own nature ordered to the generation of offspring, those who, exercising it deliberately deprive it of its natural force and power, act against nature and effect what is base and intrinsically indecent (AAS 22:559).

> The Catholic Church, to whom God himself has committed the integrity and decency of morals raises her voice aloud through our mouth, in sign of her divine mission, in order to keep the chastity of the nuptial bond free from this foul slip, and again promulgates:

> Any use whatever of marriage, in the exercise of which the act by human effort is deprived of its natural power of procreating life, violates the law of God and nature, and those who do such a thing are stained by a grave and mortal flaw (AAS 22:560).[2]

During the period of the thirties through much of the fifties, the statement of *Casti Connubii* was generally taken by Catholics as a formally infallible statement. However, as the question was raised with new urgency in the sixties, it was conceded that the

2. As quoted in Noonan, *op. cit.,* p. 427.

Pope had not spoken with such formality that it could be considered a *de fide* proposition. Thus it was possible to hope for a change in the doctrine. Although Pius XI spoke about nature and acts against nature, he did not, it should be noted, speak from a purely biological point of view. Rather he confined himself to the interpersonal communion of marriage by speaking of "the act of the spouses" and the "use of marriage." A completely biological approach would have necessitated a universal statement such as "the act of sexual partners" and the "use of sexual intercourse." I believe his statement is open to a more personalistic interpretation than is usually given it — one which will still be non-contraceptive, and I will attempt to show this in Chapter Five.

3.   Probabilism and the Pill

The medical discovery in 1953 of a progesterone pill that would make conception impossible raised a new question for moral theology. The traditional or habitual way of explaining the evil character of contraception had been an effort to show the unnatural character of the physical interference with the reproductive process at the time of intercourse. However, the Pill acted in a hidden, chemical way. It did nothing in the way of physical obstruction of the process of the sex act itself, for it had accomplished its work already by impeding ovulation. Therefore the door seemed open to arguments allowing the use of the Pill as "natural" while retaining the formal condemnation of physical, mechanical contraception.

Only two years before the development of this new form of contraception, Pius XII had reaffirmed the teaching of *Casti Connubii* in his 1951 address to the Italian Catholic Society of Midwives. He noted that Pius XI

solemnly proclaimed again the fundamental law of the marital act and relations: any attempt by the spouses in the completion of the conjugal act or in the development of its natural consequences, having the aim of depriving the act of the force inherent in it and of impeding the procreation of a new life, is immoral; and no alleged indication or need can convert an intrinsically immoral act into a moral and lawful one.

This precept is as valid today as it was yesterday; and it will be the same tomorrow and always, because it does not imply a precept of the human law, but is the expression of a law which is natural and divine (AAS 43:843).[3]

Noonan notes that "the important clause here is . . . . 'in the development of its natural consequences.' By these words, Pius XII asserted that not only did Pius XI condemn the impeding of coitus — a prohibition of coitus interruptus, the condom, and the pseudo-vagina — but he condemned such means as the douche and other post-coital efforts to destroy or expel the spermatozoa." [4] The statement was not interpreted as an *ex cathedra* definition but it was treated with great respect.

In 1958 Pius XII spoke again. In June of that year Louis Jansens argued that the theory of correcting the defaults of the natural mechanism could be used to justify the use of the anovulant Pill. Pius XII answered on September 12, 1958.

But one provokes a direct sterilization and therefore an illicit one, whenever one stops ovulation in order to preserve the uterus and the organism from the consequences of a pregnancy which they are not capable of supporting. Certain moralists assert that it is permitted to take drugs to this end, but this is a mistake. It is equally necessary to reject the opinion of several doctors and moralists who permit their use whenever a medical indication renders an early conception undesirable or in other similar cases which it would not be possible to mention here; in these cases the employment of drugs has as its end the preventing of conception in preventing ovulation; it is therefore a matter of direct sterilization.

To justify it they quote at times the moral principle, correct

---

3. *Ibid.,* p. 467.
4. *Ibid.,* p. 467.

in itself, but wrongly interpreted: "It is lawful to correct the defects of nature." Since, in practice, it suffices, in order to use this principle, to have reasonable probability, they assert that it is a matter here of correcting a natural defect. If this principle had unqualified validity, eugenics could without hesitation utilize the drug method to stop the transmission of a defective heredity. But it is still necessary to consider by what means the natural defect is corrected and to take care not to violate in any respect other principles of morality.[5]

The 1958 statement of Pius XII, though not given or received under the formality of infallibility, became the generally accepted authoritative norm regarding the Pill until 1963.

In 1963, Dr. John Rock of Boston, a Catholic physician who had helped to develop the progesterone pill, published a book [6] in which he argued for the morality of the Pill. To him it was the rational means of protecting other values in the family. His book and others introduced the period of probabilism in the contraception debate.

Either as a result of the Rock book or as a simultaneous reflection of Dutch opinion, Bishop Bekkers of 's Hertogenbosch made a television broadcast on March 21, 1963 in which he spoke of "true love, expressing itself spontaneously . . . . The Christian should draw his own conclusions from this view of marriage regarding the difficult question of birth regulation. Each technique for that purpose is somehow unsatisfactory . . . . And while we know that periodic continence is a solution for many people, we are also aware that it presents others with really insuperable obstacles." [7] Drawing attention to the Pill, he said that "Most commentators have forgotten, it appears, to ask themselves seriously whether these progestative hormone products really belong

5. *Address to the Seventh International Congress of Hematology,* AAS 50: 735-736.
6. *The Time Has Come* (New York: Alfred A. Knopf, 1963).
7. *Herder Correspondence,* October, 1963, p. 28. Also quoted in *The Pill* by Leo Pyle (Helicon, 1964), p. 6.

to the same category as the more traditional, well-known contraceptives." [8]

Since it is likely that the commentators had asked themselves
this question and answered affirmatively, Bishop Bekkers statement had the effect of denying it, thus adding theological weight
to the contraceptive use of the Pill. He was followed in this by
Mgr. J. M. Reuss and Canon Janssens in 1963, both of whom
distinguished between physical, mechanical contraception and the
Pill and favored the permissibility of the Pill. The debate was now
in full swing. The advocates of contraception could point to one,
then another, and then another respectable Catholic figure who
favored a change in the doctrine to allow contraception, at least
in the form of the Pill.

With respectable voices on both sides of the question, it seemed
to become subject to the doctrine of probabilism. According to
probabilism, if a matter is in doubt, then the person who must
make the choice should weigh the arguments advanced by both
sides and choose the side that seems the more likely. When the
law is uncertain, the presumption is for freedom. For the doctrine
of probabilism to apply, it is necessary first of all that the question
be in doubt. Thus it became necessary for the advocates of
contraception to show this doubt. The fact that a bishop and
theologians were speaking out contrary to the previous statements
of Pius XII and were not drawing down upon themselves a
condemnation from Rome was interpreted as an indication that
Rome was in a state of doubt. This was heightened by the fact
that John XXIII had appointed a special commission to investigate the problem and by the fact that Paul VI had reserved
the question from the debate of Vatican II.

Paul VI began to speak on June 23, 1964. He announced
an enlarged Papal Birth Control Commission and accompanied
his announcement with this statement:

... But meanwhile we say frankly that up to now we do

8. *Herder Correspondence,* October, 1963, p. 30. Also in Pyle, *op. cit.,* p.
   7.

not have sufficient motive to consider out of date and therefore not binding the norms given by Pope Pius XII in this
regard. Therefore they must be considered valid, at least until
we feel obliged in conscience to change them.[9]

Vatican II did not deal directly with the problem of contraception because Paul VI had reserved the question to himself.
However in the *Pastoral Constitution on the Church in the Modern
World,* the Fathers of the Council reflected the ambiguity of the
state of the question. From a personalist point of view, it held
that the parents must make the decision about future offspring
taking into consideration a number of personal factors. On the
other hand, their decision to postpone or avoid pregnancy must
make sure that any procedure is conformed to objective standards
and to the authoritative teaching of the Church.

The promulgation of *the Church in the Modern World* served
to provide more matter for debate, and ever more frequently it
became customary to speak in terms of probabilism. In this
cloudy atmosphere, Pope Paul VI spoke again addressing the
delegates of the Italian Society of Obstetrics and Gynecology on
October 29, 1966. After some remarks about the complexity of
the birth control problem, he went on to state that the magisterium
was not in doubt.

Meanwhile, as we have already said in the above mentioned discourse [23 June, 1964], the norm until now taught
by the Church, integrated by the wise instructions of the
Council, demands faithful and generous observance. It cannot
be considered not binding as if the magisterium of the Church
were in a state of doubt at the present time, whereas it is
rather in a moment of study and reflection concerning matters
which have been put before it as worthy of the most attentive
consideration.[10]

9. "The Times," June 24, 1964. Quoted by Pyle, *op. cit.,* p. 212.
10. As quoted by Leo Pyle, *Pope and Pill* (London: Darton, Longmann
    and Todd, 1968), p. 212.

Paul's statement, apparently intended to curb the application of probabilism by denying a state of doubt, brought him a torrent of bitter criticism. Even his supporters found themselves in difficulty to explain what was meant by a "moment of study and reflection" and to show how this was different from a state of doubt. It seems to me that the statement is unintelligible except as a clarification of the statement of June 23, 1964. I think that Paul wanted to change the teaching and was hoping that the contraceptive argumentation would show him the way. I think he was being perfectly honest in saying in 1964 that he didn't have sufficient grounds for a change, i.e., that the argumentation was less than convincing. By October 29, 1966, the Birth Control Commission had submitted its reports. Quite obviously, the argumentation on behalf of contraception likewise failed to convince Pope Paul VI of its own inherent value and that the official teaching could be changed. Perhaps by this time he was convinced that it was impossible for him to change the doctrine of non-contraception but that he needed further study as to how to express the doctrine in a way that would be relevant to the married couples for whom it was intended. In this light, he would want to avoid saying that the matter was in doubt, thereby giving encouragement to countless couples to practice contraception, and he could hope that in a short time he would be able to make a statement in terms relevant to the thought of our day. The statement of *Humanae Vitae* almost two years later would make it seem that in the intervening time he did not succeed in finding more relevant terms of reference but that the growing crisis forced him to come out with a repetition of the traditional philosophizing as well as the traditional doctrine.

4. The Birth Control Commission Report

The advocacy of the doctrine of probabilism was enhanced with the publication of the reports of the Birth Control Commission in April, 1967. Although the members of the Commission were pledged to secrecy, one of them let the reports out for publication. In the English speaking world, they were first published by the *National Catholic Reporter.* The division that existed among the members of the Commission and the fact that a majority of them favored a radical change in the Church's doctrine on birth control added considerable prestige to the advocates of contraception. Now their arguments could be bolstered by an appeal to authority; to be sure it wasn't the authority of the magisterium, but to many the majority decision was an authority of a tangible sort. If the Commission members appointed by the Pope didn't go along with the tradition, how could the couple in a Paris apartment or a Los Angeles subdivision be expected to abide by it? To more and more it seemed that there was a real state of doubt in the teaching of the Church.

Interestingly enough, the publication of the Birth Control Commission reports put the argumentation much more on the level of authority than on the level of rational argument about contraception itself. The so-called minority report was criticized for avoiding the issue of contraception itself and for stressing primarily the tradition of the Church's teaching and the authority of this tradition. However, since the publication of the reports, it has seemed to this observer that there has been very little praise for the argumentation of the majority position. Instead, the emphasis has been on the fact that a *majority* of the Commission recommended change. Such an emphasis is an argument for authority, pure and simple. My personal reaction to the majority position was surprise that the Pope himself had not made it public immediately. I found the argumentation unconvincing, as I explain in Chapter Four, and it seemed to me that Paul VI would have done well to share with the world immediately his reasons for being unpersuaded.

To the advocates of contraception, it now seemed that the battle was over. They had won. The practice of great numbers of Catholics had in fact changed; it was just a matter of time until the Pope gave the official seal of approval to the *de facto* change that had already taken place. There appeared to be such confidence that they had succeeded in changing the teaching of

the Church that very few bothered to meet in advance the possibility that Pope Paul would actually reaffirm the doctrine of non-
contraception in an authoritative way. Gregory Baum, O.S.A, was
an exception. He had written long before this time that "since
the conscience of the Church is so deeply divided on this issue
and since the solution is in no way contained in divine revelation, the authoritative norms which the Pope himself, as universal teacher, will propose in due time, shall not be a definitive
interpretation of divine law, binding under all circumstances,
but rather offer an indispensable and precious guide for the
Christian conscience." [11]

5. The Encyclical: *Humanae Vitae*

It became apparent that Pope Paul's statements of June,
1964 and October, 1966 did not have the intended effect of
retaining the norms of non-contraception. On the contrary, since
he had not said anything in the authoritative manner of Pius
XI and Pius XII, it became a common interpretation that the
Pope was doubtful; if *he* was in doubt, what about the rest of
the world? Probabilism was gaining such a firm foothold that
contraception could almost be argued as the *more* probable or
even more certain side of the question. Into this atmosphere,
Pope Paul VI introduced *Humanae Vitae*. Its teaching that "each
and every marriage act must remain open to the transmission
of life" (paragraph 11) clarified the aura of uncertainty regarding
the official teaching of the magisterium and triggered the most
lively reaction the Church has seen in at least 400 years.
The application of probabilism was curtailed, for no longer could
it be argued that the magisterium was in a state of doubt.

However, as with the publication of the Birth Control Commission reports in 1967, the question of authority was raised.
The arguments brought forward by the majority position were
inconclusive, but emphasis was laid on the authority of the

---

11. *Commonweal*, December 24, 1965.

Commission majority, although from the point of view of ecclesiology, it had no teaching authority. The natural law arguments used in *Humanae Vitae* were likewise inconclusive to many. Therefore, the question reverted to the authority of the Pope to teach as he did in this matter.

This chapter has only attempted to present a very quick survey of the question as it reaches us today. Several things should stand out. The tradition of the magisterium on contraception has been constant for twenty centuries. The natural law arguments of those defending the magisterium are presently failing to convince many. The personalist arguments of those advocating contraception have failed to convince many others. The debate since *Humanae Vitae* has shifted from argumentation about the meaning of the married sexual union to a debate about authority and conscience. What is clearly needed is an explanation of the meaning of marriage that will accord both with the tradition of the magisterium and with the values urged by the writers in the personalist mode. Such an effort in this direction is made in Chapter Five.

ECCLESIAL ASPECTS OF THE CONTRACEPTION CONTROVERSY

Chapter One

CAN THE CHURCH TEACH INFALLIBLY ABOUT CONTRACEPTION?

1. State of the Question

At first sight, it may seem strange to raise the question as to whether or not the Church really has anything to say about contraception considering how much the Church has said over the past centuries. One has only to leaf through John Noonan's *Contraception*[1] to realize that the Church has been in the business of teaching in this area of human behavior for some 1900 years. It may seem rather late to raise the question as to whether the Church has any competency in this field, but the question has been raised.

More precisely stated, the question is whether or not the teaching of the Church in this area ever can be definitive and infallible or whether, by the very nature of the subject, the Church's teaching will always be changeable and non-infallible.[2] Such a point of view says that it is impossible for the Pope, and/or bishops in Council, to teach infallibly in this area. That is, the

---

1. *Op. cit.*
2. "Papal infallibility has to do with what Jesus Christ taught us to believe and to do (faith and morals). But the evaluation of birth control has to do with human wisdom . . . . In this area the Church has the authority to teach but here its teaching is always non-infallible and changeable." Fr. Gregory Baum, O.S.A., *Toronto Globe and Mail*, August 1, 1968.

Church in its magisterium may have something to say in the way of human wisdom, but it has nothing to say in its unique capacity as the Body of Christ whose Head can continue to clarify revelation through the continued working of the Holy Spirit. Somehow or other the Spirit may lead each couple in truth, but that same Spirit cannot lead the Church to teach infallibly in this same area. It is an important question, and its investigation may be a fruitful first step.

It seems to me that if we are to answer in any decent form the question about the Church's competence to teach infallibly about contraception, we first have to have a clear understanding of what we mean by the Church and by its role as teacher. Then we can look at what is involved in contraception to see whether this falls within the scope of its jurisdiction.

2. The Church

That desirable, clear understanding of what we mean by the Church, however, has been obscured at the same time that the storm clouds of the contraception battle have been forming. Whether or not this is coincidental or somehow causal is beyond the scope of this book, but it is beyond question that the same five years that have seen the contraception controversy have also witnessed a growing crisis of authority within the Church. I think that for the person who is interested in the Church, this crisis of authority can be interpreted as confusion about (1) what the Church is (ecclesiology) and (2) how teaching and learning is meant to be effected in the Church (religious epistemology). Without entering into a lengthy investigation of the nature of the Church and current conceptions about it, I think we can look at four different elements in the Church today which receive various degrees of emphasis, an emphasis somewhat related to the personal standpoint of the individual concerned.

(a) *The Layman.* The contraception controversy has provided many a lay person with a situation without recent precedent for expressing his or her personal feelings about birth control and the teaching of the Popes. This has been encouraged by many who felt that since the laity formed the majority of the Church as the People of God, the lay voice needed to be heard. Furthermore, since the workings of the Holy Spirit were not limited to the magisterium, and since the teaching of the magisterium had been formed under different social conditions and seemed to be confused under the present social and scientific conditions, it was possible, probable, or even certain that the Holy Spirit was now to be heard through the very emphatic voice of the laity who were demanding a change in the official teaching. The tract of John Henry Cardinal Newman, "On Consulting the Faithful in Matters of Doctrine" has been referred to by those who emphasized the role of the laity in forming the Church. Newman's phrase, *consensus fidelium,* is almost a catchword in this emphasis for if one thing seems certain in the contraception controversy, it is that there is no consensus among the Christians of Europe and North America that the traditional doctrine is true. According to this emphasis on the laity as forming the key element in the Church, surveys that show that over 50% of the Catholics in a given area practice contraceptive birth control would indicate that the consensus of the faithful favors contraception, and this may indicate that the Holy Spirit favored it too. I will treat of this again later on in Chapter Three.

(b) *The Theologian.* A second emphasis is on the role of the theologian in the Church. It is probably the best-known fact of recent Catholic life that the birth control commission appointed by John XXIII and continued by Paul VI ended in a divided position with the majority recommending a change in the teaching to allow contraception. The next best-known fact of recent Catholic life might be that sizable numbers of Catholic theologians and philosophers (the last count was around 500) have gone on record against the papal teaching. It is not altogether clear how many of these believe that the Pope has taught wrongly, or how many merely want to say that, since he did not speak in the manner of a *de fide, ex cathedra* pronounce-

ment, there is still room to debate and to form one's own conscience without regarding the official doctrine as normative. At
any rate, whether it is expressed in so many words, the inference
is clear. How could so many learned people be wrong? How
could the Pope be right in the face of this? Is not the Pope in
error three times — once for not listening to his own commission, secondly for teaching an outmoded doctrine, and thirdly
for being a prisoner of the Curia?

(c) *The Council.* While the first emphasis on the laity leaned
on numbers, the second emphasized the expertise of theologians
and others(although the numbers aspect is certainly there.) The
third makes use both of numbers and expertise but also adds
a more dogmatic note. This is the appeal to a Council — some
2500 bishops who are supposed to have good theological advice
and personal knowledge. Moreover, in addition to numbers and
expertise, it is a matter of faith that when a Council sanctioned
by the Pope defines a matter of faith or morals, it has been led
infallibly by the Holy Spirit. In the light of the current question,
the inference in the emphasis on a Council seems to be that the
papal teaching should be appealed to a higher body — the Council.
It is well known that this was Luther's appeal. However, Luther
is much more to be excused for this appeal than any Catholic
today. Luther lived at a time of conciliarism, at a time when the
shock of the Western Schism had still not worn away. We live
with the heritage of Vatican I and Vatican II which leave no
doubt. Neither Council leaves any room for holding that it is
possible to appeal to a General Council as being above the Pope,
though it is, of course, still possible to appeal a non-defined teaching of the Pope to a Council-in-union-with-the-Pope in order to
obtain a clarification, a definition or even a change.

(d) *The Pope.* The fourth emphasis has to with the Pope
himself. Until the papal encyclical reaffirmed the traditional
teaching, both sides tended to make use of this emphasis. Those
teaching that contraception was permissible seemed to assume that
the papal authority would show that they had been right all along.

Those holding to the tradition waited anxiously for the Pope to put his authority behind them showing that they had been right. However, since the Pope spoke, matters have changed somewhat. Those holding to the tradition have been reaffirmed very strongly, but if they were hoping for a "definition" they were disappointed. Those advocating contraception were dismayed, to say the least, but they quickly rallied to point out that the Pope had not spoken *ex cathedra*. (They have been something less than quick to point out that no other matters of human actions have ever been taught *ex cathedra* either, nor have they been quick to point out that "freedom of conscience" in this one "undefined" area is the "freedom of conscience" that we have in all other "undefined" areas of human behavior.)

At any rate, advocates of both traditions — the one of 1900 years and the contraceptive tradition of the last 5 years — seem to recognize the unique role of the Pope in the Church. True, he has been severely criticized for not following the recommendations of the Commission; his teaching has been called inadequate and wrong; but the fact that such a fuss is made about *his* teaching (while little such fuss will be made about mine) is witness to the fact that there is still a belief that the Pope has a unique role in the Church and can in fact teach infallibly. To deny this formally would be to enter into formal heresy, and most theologians are avoiding this like the plague. Whether or not those who oppose the papal teaching on contraception still believe that he *could* teach infallibly in *this* area if he made his present teaching into a definition is probably known only by the Holy Spirit.

Today, then, there are these four different elements in the Church — the laity, the theologians, the bishops, and the Pope — each receiving various amounts of emphasis. All of these make up the whole Church, and exclusive emphasis on only one aspect will give a distorted picture of the whole. However, this does not mean that there is not an order created by Christ in which the voice of one, the Pope, can have more teaching weight and authority than the other elements. After all, it is worth keeping in mind that Christ did single out Peter for a unique role in the college of the apostles who together with him were given the responsibility of forming a new People of God.

Our understanding of each of these four elements in the Church points to the notion of a Church which is tangible and can be heard-— either through a survey, a vote, or a voice. None of these elements so emphasizes the Church of the Spirit as to fog over the Church of the audible and tangible flesh. Thus when the Church teaches, it is always in a visible, tangible, and materially specific way.

As we asked before, what about the Church teaching about contraception? Does the Church, in its unique capacity as God's pilgrim people, have anything more than human wisdom to offer on this subject? In other words, is contraception a proper subject for its infallible teaching authority (which can be exercised by the ordinary magisterium as well as by the extraordinary magisterium of formal definitions)? Perhaps a quick look at the relationships of the magisterium of the Church to some of the other facets of Christian life that are involved in the contraception controversy will make it more believable that the subject of contraception does indeed fall within the special teaching competence of Christ's Church.

3.   Facets of Christian Life

(a) *Love.* No one needs another book today to tell him or her that Christ gave us a law of love. If the writing and the catechizing of the last few years have made one point, it has been that Jesus taught us to love one another. This is a need of every age and perhaps especially so in any age which tends to intellectualization. However the emphasis in itself doesn't answer man's needs; he wants to know, "What do you mean by love?" Is each man to be his own judge on what love is? That is, is it up to each man's conscience to be the *ultimate* (as distinguished from the *proximate*) source of knowing what love is and what it isn't?

The Christian says that he believes that Jesus came to reveal

what love means in the human form. His whole life was a
revelation of what love means, and he left us with the commandment to love one another as he himself has loved us. However,
even this doesn't fully satisfy, for we want to know more about
love as it took place in the humanity of Christ and as it is
meant to take place in our own humanity. Does the commandment
of love mean that we are to have affective feelings toward our
fellow man, especially towards him who has injured us or whom
we fear, perhaps for very good reasons? Does it mean that unique
self-giving love called *agapé* in the New Testament, or does
it mean the affection of friendship (*philia*), or does it mean
eros, despite the fact that the New Testament never uses this
latter term? We know that Jesus forgave his enemies from the
cross, but how did he *feel* towards them? How did he feel towards
the hypocrites and the dishonest money changers?

These are questions which are both interesting and important
to the person who is serious about his relationship with Christ.
I would not attempt to answer them here, for my point is rather
limited. I only want to show that any specific act which is meant
to express love in a human manner would seem to fall within
the scope of how Jesus, and hence his Church, teaches us to act.
Certainly no one is going to challenge that sexual intercourse is
meant to be such an act.

(b) *Sex.* If the sex act were merely a matter of biology or physiology, then it would be very difficult for me to see how it would
come within the scope of Christian revelation. I could envisage
it coming within the scope of the Church's teaching authority
only insofar as everything else concerned with the body can be
looked at from the point of view of the preservation of life which
in turn seems to flow from the fifth commandment in some way.
Furthermore, the reader of the Gospel will not find Jesus giving
him any biology lessons.

However, Jesus does teach about sex. His teaching about
marriage and divorce was so radical that it astonished his hearers
who found it so strict and such an infringement on their idea of
freedom that it seemed better not to get married in the first

place (Mt 19:10). In the Sermon on the Mount, a passage which in its entirety is seen frequently as a promulgation in some detail of the commandment of love, he teaches that "every one who looks at a woman lustfully has already committed adultery with her in his heart" (Mt 5:28). Without a doubt this quotation has been the source of considerable anguish to a great many men and women who have struggled and been concerned with "impure thoughts." To say that these people have frequently misunderstood the images which flit across the imagination of almost everyone who has blood in their veins and confused them with the actual desire of lust for an illicit relationship is to state a truism but still does not do away with their anguish. If Jesus had not taught this, and/or if the biblical writers had not included this, perhaps a great amount of human suffering could have been avoided. I think this is relevant to the present case in which Pope Paul VI is being criticized for the hardship that his teaching will bring to people who possibly could have had a much easier and "fuller" life if they had been permitted to go on in ignorance and "good faith."

St. Paul in Romans 1, Galatians 5 and 1 Corinthians 5, 6, and 7 is also rather obviously concerned with sexual behavior. His letters to the Romans and Galatians are sometimes called the epistles of Christian liberty, and it seems to me that Paul's concern with sexual matters in these epistles is a reflection of his greater concern about what freedom means. The understatement of the year would be that St. Paul didn't think that authentic Christian freedom was achieved by following the course of passion or by doing anything that seemed to be fulfilling at the moment. The chapters in 1 Corinthians stand somewhat by themselves, but they can also be seen in the larger context of an epistle that deals with gifts of the Spirit, including the gift of overcoming universal temptations (Ch. 10) and climaxing with the gift of love and the resurrection. Thus it seems to me that Paul's teaching about sex in this letter is part of his concern with what it means to be authentically Christian and responsive to the Holy Spirit.

The more one emphasizes that sexual intercourse is meant

to be an authentic expression by two persons of their mutual love — the personalist approach — the more important it is that he have an authentically Christian understanding about love. An approach to sex which is heavily biological or concerned with marriage rights and duties with little talk about love would not seem, on the other hand, to require a truly Christian understanding of love.

Contraception reflects something about what one thinks about sex and love. Christ and the sacred authors also thought and taught about sex and love. Thus I cannot help but conclude that contraception falls within the scope of the Church's mission of preaching the gospel and applying its message of love.

(c) *Sacrament.* Marriage is a sacrament which involves love and, normally speaking, sex. So important is marriage in our consideration of love and sex that one of the most important criteria by which we judge the moral value of sexual intercourse is the presence or absence of the marriage contract between the two people involved. I intend to develop this more thoroughly in Chapter Five, but for the present I only wish to state that since Christ has raised marriage to the level of a sacrament, this would be one more reason for urging that contraception falls within the scope of the infallible teaching authority of his Church.

(d) *Grace.* Every time a priest preaches to his people, either from the pulpit or in writing, about contraception and tells them that it is never a sin not to do the impossible, he is saying something about temptation, suffering and God's grace. He is saying something about his view of man in his fallen and redeemed state, his view of man who is called to share in the resurrection of Jesus and Mary by ascending Calvary with them.

Undoubtedly, the Catholic doctrine on contraception calls for great faith and willingness to walk with Christ in his earthly sojourn as well as in his resurrected glory. Living out this doctrine of Christ's Church is going to demand from many people that they really believe that "God is faithful, and he will not let you be tempted beyond your strength, but with the temptation will also provide the way of escape that you may be able to endure it" (1 Cor 10:13). To the extent that you bring in the possibility or impossibility of living out the doctrine of non-contraception, you are bringing in the doctrine of grace. It seems to me that much of the argumentation on behalf of contraception has dealt with the impossibility of couples living in any other way in the present sociological framework. The relation of this doctrine to the doctrine of grace is one more reason for including it within the scope of the infallible teaching authority of the Church.

(e) *Sin and Change of Heart.* The reactions to Pope Paul's encyclical include comments such as, "If contraception is sinful, well then, I guess we're just going to be sinners," and, "I'll give up the Church before I give up the pill." The quotations are not direct, but I think they fairly express the contents of some of the reactions carried in the press in the early weeks after the encyclical. Such comments say much about the willingness of people to undergo a change, a conversion, about their basic moral option, about what is really their god, about what they think of Christ's Church and salvation. Such comments say much more about these things than they do about contraception itself. Again the reason for including these matters is that they provide one more reason for including contraceptive birth control within the scope of the infallible teaching authority of the Church which certainly must continue to promulgate the clear teaching of Jesus about the necessity of a change of heart.

Whether we look at each one of these elements in the contraception issue singly or all together, it seems unavoidable to conclude that we have an issue here which is within the competence of the Church teaching in her unique capacity as the infallible voice of Christ on earth today. It may seem that I have been belaboring the obvious, but when such an important question has been raised, it should be answered in at least a little detail. When a statement is made that puts an important area of moral behavior completely beyond the scope of the Church's unique, infallible teaching competence and authority I think it is necessary to reply with something more than a quip that such a statement is a gratuitous assertion.

I am not prepared to state categorically that the Church has taught infallibly on contraceptive birth control within marriage. It is agreed by all that the Church has *not defined* anything in this area, that is, that she has not yet taught with her *extraordinary* magisterium through a conciliar or papal *ex cathedra* statetment. Whether or not the constant exercise of her ordinary magisterium throughout nineteen centuries to forbid contraception (in answer to a question that has been raised in a number of ways) constitutes an infallible use of the ordinary magisterium is a good theological question and one that may possibly be answered definitively some day. In the meantime it is erroneous and simplistic to write off the whole question by putting it outside the area in which the Church *can* teach infallibly. Such teaching would carry with it the further danger of denying a formal definition if and when the issue is ever forced to be clarified in that way, and such a denial in those circumstances would be heresy.

Chapter Two

THEOLOGY AND THE CHURCH

1. The Role of Theology

In trying to attain some perspective on the contraception controversy, we are faced with trying to evaluate the various "people factors." These are the actors in the drama. Their importance is such that after the publication of *Humanae Vitae* most of the attention became focused on a few controversialists while the issue of contraception itself lay relatively untouched. In this chapter, we will take a look at the role of theology in the Christian faith, then examine the role of the theologian in the contraception controversy and finally make a critique of some of the theologizing and philosophizing that has been done in order to justify the practice of contraception.

(a) *Theology and Faith*. As a teacher of theology, I have had the uncomfortable experience of talking with students who were taking a course so that they could have more knowledge and *less* faith. They seemed to be thinking that "faith" was for the unlearned and that as soon as they became learned, their faith would be replaced by understanding and comprehension. Their approach to religion was much the same as would be their approach to any other "problem" area of twentieth century life.

The study of theology, however, does differ from other organized areas of knowledge and it is not identical with philosophy.

Since the theologian and the philosopher, however, do deal with many of the same areas of life, its nature, ends and problems, etc., it might be well to make a brief comparison of at least these two fields of thought.

The work of a philosopher is judged on an empirical basis. The philosopher must first of all be an acute observer of all that is and he must do his best to relate it. He forms his premises, and from these he draws his conclusions. His conclusions are judged (or should be) *entirely* on how well they are contained in his premises, and his premises are open for all other philosophers to criticize. The philosopher does not and cannot ask us to believe him. He has to be able to prove the correctness of his premises and his conclusions, and he only asks us to reason with him. It is this process of formulation and criticism, reformulation and reasoned debate that forms the basis for the dialogue of philosophers and keeps their magazines and publishers in business. It is healthy and necessary.

The Christian believer on the other hand does not approach something (or better yet, someone) he believes with the same critical and even skeptical attitude as the philosopher approaches a philosophical conclusion. The Christian believer believes that somehow the one creative God has revealed himself through the prophets and finally in Jesus Christ. He believes the "something" of his faith solely because the Someone has revealed it.[1] He does not demand proof from God, for to do so would amount to saying that God wasn't believable on his own word but had to approach us in the same way as any one of the philosophers.

However, the believer still seeks to understand as much as possible. He likes to think about what God has revealed. He wants to know what it means for him; he wants to know how one aspect of God's revelation is related to another; he wants to know if

---

1. This is not the place to explore current theories of revelation. However, I think it is fair to say that except for the radical immanentists, those who stress the   individual's perception of God revealing himself here and now generally acknowledge the necessity of objectifying that experience into "something" that can be said about the "Someone revealing himself."

he can or must draw from this revelation some conclusions, which are not themselves the primary "something revealed" but seem to flow from it.

As he begins thinking about his faith he becomes a theologian in the sense that every believer who has ever thought about his religion is a theologian. Theology, after all, in the classic and still valid definition, is simply faith seeking understanding. It does not seek to *replace* one's faith but rather to enlighten it, to show the unity among its various parts or facets, and hopefully to deepen it.

The professional theologian differs from the ordinary inquiring believer not in kind but rather by degree and intensity. He devotes time, perhaps his full time, to the study of his faith. He is aware that whenever someone begins to think about anything, he does so in terms of his own background. He therefore seeks to learn from the theologians of the past, filter out that which has a timeless value and to leave behind that which was only a reflection of the mode of their day. This, of course, is tricky business, for the theologian of today is just as much a prisoner of the thought patterns of his times as was the theologian of yesteryear. For this reason, even if for no other, there will never be an end to theology. The theologian brings to bear whatever is useful from the other sciences and attempts to enlarge the frontiers of theological knowledge and religious understanding.

(b) *Different Disciplines.* Within the field of theology there is the necessity for both specialized analysis and coherent synthesis. We need our scripture scholars, our catechists, our dogmatic and moral theologians, etc. We also need speculative theologians who try to weld the analytic segments into a unified synthesis.

Among the actors in the drama over *Humanae Vitae* the scripture scholars have held key roles. Their recent re-interpretation of certain biblical passages in the light of current research very definitely added fuel to the debate. Let us take a look at one of these as an example. Genesis 38:6-10 relates the account of Onan who had intercourse with his deceased brother's wife but withdrew before ejaculation and spilled his semen on the ground in order that he would not beget a child of this woman. For the sake of convenience here is the text:

> And Judah took a wife for Er his first-born, and her name was Tamar. But Er, Judah's first-born was wicked in the sight of the Lord; and the Lord slew him. Then Judah said to Onan, Go in to your brother's wife, and perform the duty of a brother-in-law to her, and raise up off-spring for your brother. But Onan knew that the offspring would not be his; so when he went in to his brother's wife he spilled the semen on the ground, lest he should give offspring to his brother. And what he did was displeasing in the sight of the Lord, and he slew him also.

Until just recently, it was common for scripture commentators and moral theologians to speak of the sin of Onan as being the sin of contraception, specifically coitus interruptus. Today the common interpretation holds that there is nothing in Scripture which says anything directly about contraception. Onan was guilty only of the sin of disobeying the law of the Levirate which called for a childless widow's brother-in-law to "raise up seed for the deceased brother that his name be not blotted out of Israel."

Both teachings leave certain unanswered questions. With regard to the non-contraceptive interpretation, why was the law of the Levirate not mentioned? Was it thought that the two interpretations were mutually exclusive? With regard to the interpretation which stresses only the infraction of the Levirate, if this law were so important that it's violation was deemed by God worthy of death, why do we find so little trace of it later on in the Old Testament and none at all in the New? More to the point is the fact that in the statement of the law in Deuteronomy 25:5-10 the punishment for its violation is clearly stated. After the due process of talking it over first of all with the elders who then counseled the reluctant brother-in-law, if she is still denied her due, the aggrieved widow is to "take the sandal off his foot, spit in his face, and pronounce the following words, 'This is what we do to the man who does not restore his brother's house', and the man shall be surnamed in Israel, House-of-the-Unshod" (25: 9-10). All this was to be done in the presence of the elders.

Now all of that might be very embarrasing to a man, but it gives no indication that the violation of the Levirate was thought worthy of death either by God or by the Jews. To return to the account of Onan and Tamar, we notice that in this account Onan's father, Judah, and his brother, Shelah, are likewise shown to be violating the law of the Levirate, for Judah does not tell his son Shelah to give child to Tamar nor does he himself fulfill this obligation towards her. Why are neither Judah nor Shelah punished for violating the same law with the same woman in the same historical circumstances? The fact that they violated the Levirate but were not punished leads me to the opinion that it is simplistic to state that Onan's sin was *just* the violation of the Levirate. From the point of view of biblical studies, the question is raised as to why some later redactor did not reconcile the promulgation of the Levirate law in Deuteronomy 25 with the alleged punishment in Genesis 38 if the early generations of the Israelites had believed that Onan's sin was simply that of violating the Levirate. In brief then, the twofold context of the account of Onan's sin — both the promulgation of the law and the singling out of Onan when more than one was guilty of the violation — leaves me unsatisfied with the "solely Levirate" interpretation of the sin of Onan.

I think we have to look farther, and I would suggest that it is *the way in which* Onan violated the Levirate that made his sin especially despicable. Onan went through the motions of the life-giving act but refused to accept the consequences. He withdrew in order that the act could carry no reproductive consequences. Or, to put it in terms which will be developed later in this book, he went through the motions of the Levirate covenant, but he denied the reality of that covenant. He made a mockery of it.

I would further suggest that this harmonizes well with the instance in the New Testament where we find an unusually sudden death.

Acts 5:1-11 relates the unhappy dishonesty of Ananias and his wife Sapphira. Ananias indicated his desire to take part in the early Christian practice of selling property and giving the proceeds to the Church. However, when the actual time came for him to turn over his proceeds, he went through the motions but made certain reservations. He pretended to engage in an act of love, but he distorted it by refusing to give the "all" that this love-act required; his reservation of a hidden part for himself was dishonest, and thus he was punished by death. In terms of a covenant, I would describe this practice of giving as a covenant which required honesty in giving. If a man said he sold a field for a hundred dollars and was giving the total proceeds, whereas he had really received a hundred and fifty, his act of giving was vitiated by dishonesty and failed to meet the criteria of an act of love. Ananias engaged in this act which was meant to be a covenantal act of love, but his self-reservation distorted it; he denied the real and complete consequences of the covenantal act.

The point in looking at these passages was to illustrate how the roles of the various theological disciplines are inter-related. In this particular case the scripture scholar has to give an interpretation to the text which can likewise be applicable to similar texts regarding similar situations. The speculative theologian must try to relate this interpretation to other aspects of God's self-revelation and his covenant with men; the moral theologian, to relate all of it to Christ's call to fidelity and perfection. The dogmatic theologian has the responsibility of assigning a degree of certainty to all the conclusions, scriptural, dogmatic, and moral that are drawn from the work of these other specialists. It may sound rather intricate, it may not work this way in practice most of the time, but if it can serve to point up the complexity of theological study about contraception, then it has served its purpose. If one thing should become apparent, it is that a journalistic approach to the problem is no answer. Nor is it going to get us very far to insinuate that "everybody" holds the same position and that anybody who doesn't simply isn't with it. "Everybody" has held a lot of popular ideas which didn't stand up to repeated cross-examination and which have since been discarded.

It must be repeated that the Christian theologian starts from a position of faith. To the degree that various segments of Christianity have different faiths there will also be different theologies. Even given the same faith in essentials, say by two Catholic theologians, there will still be different theologies due to different philosophical, cultural and personal viewpoints. Between Catholic and Protestant, and between differing Protestants, there will be different theologies stemming from critical differences in faith about the basic relationship between God and man, man's present ability to keep God's law, the authority of the Bible, and the authority of the Church. The Catholic theologian accepts as true what the Catholic Church teaches definitively and he gives an assent of a lesser degree of faith to what the Catholic Church teaches authoritatively but has not yet defined. He believes that the Church is guided by the Holy Spirit in its teaching. He believes that the strength of the teaching lies not so much in the reasoning process which led to the conclusion as it does in the power of the Holy Spirit to teach through the Church despite the philosophical and theological shortcomings of the human element in the Church. This is why a theologian, and any believer for that matter, can accept a teaching of the Church but disagree with the theologizing which is purported to show the validity of that teaching. This I think is extremely important and equally relevant to the contraception controversy.

If Pope Paul had chosen to *define* the doctrine of non-contraception, many theologians would have a clear case of dogma they would accept on their faith in the Holy Spirit's guidance of the Church *and* theologizing with which they disagreed. With the present level of teaching authority being used, the theologian is not required to give the highest degree of the assent of faith. The question of what degree of assent he should give is presently debated. The *Dogmatic Constitution on the Church* of Vatican

II spoke of the "religious assent" of the soul. "This religious submission of will and of mind must be shown in a special way to the authentic teaching authority of the Roman Pontiff, even when he is not speaking *ex cathedra*" (Par. 25). The so-called "theology of dissent" that was revived in the year following the issuance of *Humanae Vitae* points out previous historical examples of dissent and claims that, in the present controversy, a person may dissent from both internal and external acceptance of the doctrine if he thinks he has sufficient reasons for doing so. It remains to be seen how the theology of dissent will avoid the result that gave rise to the cliché about every man becoming his own Pope.

It is important, too, to point out that, given the traditional conviction that a religious teaching is not dependent for its claim to assent solely on its philosophical defense, it is necessary for those who dissent to do more than cite the alleged defects in the premises stated by the teaching authority. They must also show that their own philosophical premises are not equally or even more seriously defective. Given a belief in the guidance of the Church by the Holy Spirit, there is a presumption of truth that must be given to the authoritative doctrine of the Church, and the burden of proof falls upon those who would challenge it.

2.   The Role of the Theologian

Sometimes it is easier to say what someone's role is *not,* rather than to specify what it is, and I think that this applies quite well to the role of the theologian in the contraception controversy. Thus at the outset, before I attempt to state what the theologian should be doing, I'll try to mention some of the pitfalls he should avoid.

(a) *Vigilance.* First of all the theologian is not a politician and he should not engage in demagoguery. He must be extremely aware of all the conscious and unconscious pressures being brought to bear on him to advocate contraception, and he should be extremely vigilant to avoid teaching something simply because that is what many want to hear. In the same vein he should be wary of grand-standing, making a big play for public opinion.

(b) *Charity.* Another approach that we can get along without is that which suggests that the adherents to the authoritative teaching of the Church must thereby suggest that other are corrupt. For example, one theologian has written that "it is difficult to explain how a rule of life that is based on natural law and hence corresponds to the universal moral experience of man is advocated in the present culture only by the Catholic Church, unless one wanted to suggest that the consciences of other men and even other Churches are so corrupt that they are no longer in touch with the foundation of human morality." [2]

(c) *Consistency.* A third pitfall for the theologian to avoid is talking out of both sides of his mouth. That is, he should not quote the "experience of the laity" as an experience of virtue in one area of morality and then use the "experience of the laity" as an example of sin in another. To be specific, the argument from the experience of some of the laity who see no wrong in their use of contraceptives has been used frequently in the debate. At the same time however, theologians tell us that we are living in a "post-Christian" society. We are reminded that these same Christians for whom contraception is loving behavior are likewise guilty of racism and that collectively they refuse to give even one per cent of their gross national product to help the poor and starving. One wonders at the consistency of calling these Christians experts on what constitutes authentic love within marriage and blind on what it means to love our neighbor outside the context of marriage.

---

2. Father Gregory Baum, O.S.A., in the newspaper article previously cited. Of more importance than authorship is the fact that such a statement reflects badly and unfairly on those Catholics who not only adhere to the teachings of the Holy Father on contraception but likewise follow him in his example of charity. Our Blessed Lord himself gave us the norm when he told us to "judge not." It is applicable even here.

(d) *Objectivity.* Fourthly, theologians must at least try to avoid the pick and choose method of using the social sciences. This is most difficult, perhaps psychologically impossible in controversy, for the debater soon seeks to make points instead of simply searching for the truth. For example, the advocate of contraception should not limit himself to quoting philosophers, sociologists, or psychologists who describe the harmful effects of tension in our lives. He should also quote those philosophers, sociologists, and psychologists who believe that tension is a necessary part of becoming human, who teach that only in situations of anguish, or "shipwreck," or stress do we come to grips with ourselves, the meaning of our lives, and our relationship with God.

(e) *Scholarship.* As a fifth point, in the theologian's current emphasis on anthropology, he must avoid forming a firm conclusion on the tentative and partial insights of one or more of the social sciences. The social sciences are in a state of continuing development; they are subject to fads; what seems beyond question today may be discarded as obsolete tomorrow. To form a theology on this is to build on shifting sand.

(f) *Humility.* Then he should avoid the belief in his own personal infallibility; he should avoid becoming so attached to the tradition of the last five years and perhaps his own pulpit and confessional pronouncements that he cannot change and he should avoid concluding that vocal theologians have replaced the Pope.

If the theologian who takes up the task of clarifying the contraception controversy manages to avoid these things and other pitfalls, what should he be doing in a more positive vein? Again, these are my personal reflections; I am not quoting eminent authorities! I can only appeal to common sense.

(g) *Openness.* I believe that the theologian in his search for the truth should develop the "both this . . . and this" approach. No heresy has ever started with sheer negation. Rather, they

all began with an emphasis on the truth — but only one aspect
of the truth. That aspect became more and more emphasized
until at last there came a formal denial of some other aspect of
the total truth. In the contraception controversy, if a theologian
finds himself strongly advocating one aspect, he should be asking
himself if he is actually denying another valid aspect of the truth.

(h) *Loyalty*. The theologian of today, simply because he is
a theologian and not a philosopher, must give his qualified assent
to the magisterium. He cannot brush off 19 centuries of anti-
contraceptive teaching with glib phrases about a new culture or
a new understanding of man. Now that Pope Paul has reaffirmed
the tradition in an authoritative way, the theologian is required
to give the presumption of truth to the tradition. If he is disposed
to seek its change, he must realize that the burden of proof is
upon him rather than upon the philosophy or the theology of
Humanae Vitae.

(i) *Perception*. The theologian should be perceptive and judge
things in their proper perspective. He must place his search for
the meaning of sexual morality in marriage within the framework
of the larger search for a better explanation of the total meaning
of man. Is it not simply double-talk to tell us that the *anawim*,
God's poor, will inherit the kingdom of God and then to tell us
that a justifying reason for contraception is that it will enable us
to avoid becoming poor as a result of our faith that non-contraception is God's will?

He must place the explanation of sexual morality in marriage
within the context of the call to perfection that Christ extends
to married people. He must place the search for the meaning
of sexual interpersonal relationships in the context of the Incarnation and in the context of the interpersonal relationships
of the Triune God in whose image man is created and is meant
to live.

He should try to keep his theologizing about married sexual
morality within the context of all sexual morality. This he has
not always done. What we have witnessed in the contraception

controversy is a reasoning process that has gone something like this: "Now that we've shown that we were wrong in the past about contraception, the presumption is that we were possibly (or probably) wrong about some other areas of sexuality in the present," or "We showed that non-contraception was wrong because it interfered with the spontaneous expression of love. By the same token, isn't the ban on pre-marital relations a similar interference with the spontaneous expression of love? And what about so called extra-marital relations between two people who are truly loving toward each other, who want to help each other overcome loneliness, frustration and a sense of emptiness? We used to call this adultery when we had a static concept of man's nature and his inter-personal relationships. But now, with our new understanding of man's dynamic nature and the self-determining of his own relationships, might it not be better to say that these two temporary lovers are more virtuous in their love-making, in their self-structured relationship of affective love, than they would be with their own spouses in their static contractual marriages? If we were wrong on contraception, we may be just as wrong about everything else in the sexual sphere."

Needless to say this is not the specific quote of any particular author. Nor, on the other hand, is it just a straw man. It rather seems to me to be a pretty fair representation of some of the current Catholic thinking on sex.[3] I disagree with it completely, preferring to approach the question from a different direction entirely. That is, since I believe that the evil of adultery and for-nication is revealed much more clearly than the evil of contra-ception, I prefer to look for the quality that makes the former

---

3. I am aware that Bernard Häring and some others disavow this. However, in reading their disavowals, I cannot help but conclude that their asser-tions fail to block the logical flow of the conclusions from the premises from which they argue. This is one reason I think that the phenomeno-logical approach with its expression in personalism has some severe limitations in providing the answer to the current problems in moral theology. That I feel that it has some definite value, nonetheless, is seen from the fact that the chief argument of this book is founded on a form of personalism.

an evil and then to see if this quality is also relevant to contraception. I think that the evil central to all is the denial of a covenant, and I try to develop this in Chapters Five and Six.

(j) *Practicality.* The theologian in this area should also be working to develop a better understanding of the entire moral order. In doing so, he must be aware — critically aware — that any principles that he develops and advocates to support a particular conclusion will likewise be used in other areas of human morality. Thus, principles which are over-extended to "solve" the contraception controversy can be expected to be applied in their erroneously over-extended position to other matters, especially those dealing with sex and human life. Therefore, once again the burden of proof is on the contraceptive theologian to prove his position in such a way that it is both internally consistent and does not advocate or use moral principles in such a way that they will wreck havoc when applied to other areas of human relationships.

Chapter Three

THE PEOPLE OF GOD

In his recent book, *Coresponsibility in the Church,*[1] Cardinal Suenens offers his opinion that the most fruitful discovery of Vatican II for pastoral theology is that the whole Church is the People of God. From this flows the consequence that all the members, each in his respective role, are coresponsible for the mission of the Church, and that no "role" is totally *separate* from the rest.

The advocates of contraception have frequently called attention to the fact that many of God's people do not believe that contraception is wrong; from this they argue that since the Spirit leads God's people, we should be open to the Spirit and formally change the teaching of the Church to correspond with the belief and practice of many of its members. It would seem quite important to investigate the value of this argument.

The concept of the entire Church as the People of God is solidly rooted in Scripture, and it seems expedient to look to Scripture for a better understanding of the implications of being a member of God's people.

---

1. Leon J. Cardinal Suenens, *Coresponsibility in the Church* (New York: Herder & Herder, 1969).

1.   The People of God: Old Covenant

(a) *The Beginnings.* Although the beginnings of Jewish belief
go back to Abraham who is still regarded as the father of both
Jews and Christians, it is with Moses that we see the real formation of a recognizable nation, a People of God. Moses was the
organizer, the law-giver, the greatest of the prophets, and Moses
had problems. A cursory look at the Mosaic beginnings will be
sufficient to illustrate that even from the outset the doctrine of
the "People of·God" has been a two-edged sword.

The sacred author of the Book of Exodus tells that the first
announcement to the world that Yahweh had a special people
was greeted with derision by the world powers (the Pharoah). It
immediately brought hardship upon the people as they were forced
to try to make the same number of bricks while now supplying
their own straw. Their fellow Hebrew foremen found themselves
in a difficult position and complained bitterly to Moses and Aaron.
"The Lord look upon you and judge," they said to them. "You
have made us offensive in the sight of Pharaoh and his servants,
and have put a sword into their hand to kill us."

Moses in turn passed on the complaint. "Lord," he said to
him, "Why hast thou done evil to this people? Why didst thou
ever send me?" (Ex 5:19-23).

The sacred author then shows us that the people "turned
Moses off" because of their hardships. "Moses spoke thus to
the people of Israel but they did not listen to Moses, because of
their broken spirit and their cruel bondage" (Ex 6:2-9).

The sacred author continues to show us the problems of the
People of God. The ancient equivalent of "Better Red than dead"
is expressed by a worried people, "Better to work for the Egypt-
ians than die in the wilderness" (Ex 14:12). After the deliver-
ance through the "sea of reeds," the people danced, but shortly
the complaint began again. First it centered on water. So Yahweh
gave them water (Ex 15:25). Then they complained about the
lack of food so Yahweh fed them with quail and manna (Ex 16).
Then the people lost heart and built for themselves a more visible
religious symbol, the golden calf, thereby breaking their covenant

promise. Later on, the author of Numbers recounts the reconnais-
sance of the land of Canaan. It was a land of milk and honey
but also filled with big people and fortified cities. "And the
people wept that night. And all the people of Israel murmured
against Moses and Aaron; the whole congregation said to them
'Would that we had died in the land of Egypt! Or would that we
had died in this wilderness! Why does the Lord bring us into
this land, to fall by the sword? Our wives and our little ones
will become a prey; would it not be better for us to go back
to Egypt?' And they said to one another, 'Let us choose a
captain, and go back to Egypt' " (Nb 14:1-4).[2]

From the very beginning the People of God proved to be
a very "human" people. When we read the account of the exodus
we actually wonder about their lack of "religion." The reader
of the Book of the Covenant and other sections finds lists of
sins prohibited that may well leave him astonished that a "People of God" would even think of such things. Certainly the
average parent today in instructing his children wouldn't think
of telling them to avoid sexual relations with animals, but it's
all there for the people of the Old Covenant.

Also, from the very beginning, there was a problem of faith
in God and the corresponding problem of faithfulness to him.
The practical problems looked so great, so insurmountable, so
very real, and tangible, connected as they were with their very
survival. Why this life of faith? Why this necessity of trusting Yahweh when they could have food and drink back in Egypt? Security
in Egypt? Yes, at the price of their freedom and at great cost
and risk to their faith!

These, then, are the beginnings of the People of God as seen
through the eyes of sacred authors. The people, though God's
people, are still very much people in this world and of this world.
Their interest is in the "now" — today's food and drink, today's
security, and tomorrow was not considered in the light of an

---

2. The precise historicity of the accounts of the exodus will not be considered here. The point of recalling them is to show that the sacred
   authors regularly view the People of God as less than faithful to Yahweh.

after-life but simply in terms of physical needs and expectations. Faith was planted but very much in need of constant nourishment in the way of signs and wonders showing the providential and saving character of their God.

(b) *Through the Eyes of the Prophets.* One has to be careful when speaking about the people as seen through the eyes of the prophets, for there were prophets and prophets. We have to distinguish between the popular prophets and the classical prophets whose works have reached us in the Scriptures. In the middle of the eighth century before Christ, the word prophet had the connotation of someone attached officially to the temple; his message was invariably one pleasing to the people. So heavy was this connotation that when Amaziah, the priest of Bethel told Amos to leave, Amos replied, "I was no prophet, neither did I belong to any of the brotherhoods of prophets" (Am 7: 14). The message of Amos was blunt, clear and unpleasant: This people is a sinful people. Change! Come back to the Lord or your enemies will overtake you. When Jeremiah over a century later began prophesying to submit to Nebuchadnezzar, he was opposed by Hananiah who prophesied peace and immediate restoration. Jeremiah replied, "The prophets who preceded you and me, from ancient times prophesied war, famine, and pestilence against many countries and great kingdoms. As for the prophet who prophesies peace, when the word of that prophet comes to pass, then it will be known that the Lord has truly sent the prophet" (Jr 28:8-9). The verdict of Scripture is that the prophets of peace, the propagators of the status quo, the Amaziahs and Hananiahs were false prophets, and so we are led to look at the People of God through the eyes of less sanguine men, the men who had the unpopular calling to be a prophet of Yahweh.

Three elements in the prophetic message are particularly relevant to our time and to the discussion of the total picture in which the contraception controversy is situated.

(1) The first of these is the fact that the People of God is a covenanted and *therefore* sinful people. The prophetic message lays heavy emphasis on the fact that this people is a covenanted

people. It is their violation of the covenant which makes them so sinful to Yahweh. Objectively speaking their actions weren't much different from those of their neighbor, and that is precisely the trouble. Yahweh, however, has called them to a higher way of life, a life of faith in him, fidelity to him, and humaneness to their fellow man.

> Hear this word that the Lord has spoken against you,
> O people of Israel, against the whole family which I brought
> up out of the land of Egypt:
> 'You only have I known
> of all the families of the earth;
> therefore I will punish you
> for all your iniquities' (Am 3:1-2).

The same message is found running through all the prophetic works. A particularly beautiful passage shows the fatherhood of God contrasted with the consequences of rejecting his care,

> When Israel was a child, I loved him,
> And out of Egypt I called my son.
> The more I called them, the more they went
>   from me; . . .
> They shall return to the land of Egypt
> And Assyria shall be their king,
> because they have refused to return to me (Ho 11:1, 2, 5).

The sin of Israel was that it had abandoned Yahweh, it had deserted the covenant. Hosea relates this desertion to the marriage covenant and could scarcely speak in stronger terms: ". . . the land commits great harlotry by forsaking the Lord" (Ho 1:2).

(2) The second element in the prophetic message worth noting is the people's rejection of authentic reform. This rejection of the covenant was not accomplished in so many words. That is, the people didn't sign a petition or take a vote formally rejecting Yahweh as their God. It was their actions that spoke; indeed their words could and did remain very "religious."

The covenant bound them together as one people, a brotherhood. They were to love their neighbor; at the least, they were not to harm him. But what do we find in the prophets? We find as sorry a catalogue of injustices to one's fellow man as we would want to find anywhere. Slavery, oppression of the poor, prostitution, refusal to give a hearing to a man who had a grievance, getting rich through the exploitation of the weak, bribery, legal injustices, and the women caring only for their drink, encouraging their husbands to exploit others in their business dealings.

All of this was condemned repeatedly by the prophets, and they in turn were called troublemakers and accordingly rejected. The prophets, however, were not just negative; they pleaded passionately for reform, for a return to Yahweh, for a renewal of trust in him and a sense of brotherhood toward their fellow man. In spite of their efforts authentic reform was consistently rejected.

(3) A third important element has to do with liturgical reform. One of the earliest and best known of such reforms was that of King Josiah (640-609 B.C.). It was aimed at destroying the idolatry that plagued Israel and 2 Kings 23 relates how Josiah set about eliminating the idolatrous shrines and sanctuaries throughout the country. For his work in this regard, he received one of the three favorable mentions by the historians of the kings in Scripture. Aside from the resentment that he earned from the priests who were now unemployed as a result of his liturgical reform, Josiah did not seem to stir up much popular feelings one way or the other. It was an external reform; it didn't require an inner change; it was imposed by force by the king.

The prophets, too, were interested in liturgical reform. It was their constant and unpleasant task to chastize the people for their false, idolatrous worship and to call them back to the worship of Yahweh. However, when it came to the worship of God, they were interested in authentic worship.

The people on the other hand found it easier to concentrate on fulfilling the letter of the law in carrying out their liturgical duties. They could assign to these practices a real "religious" value in their own right regardless of personal dispositions. It

took a man like the prophet Amos to provide them with the
stinging, classical reminder that liturgy which was just external
was unprofitable for the soul.

I hate, I despise your feasts,
and I take no delight in your solemn assemblies.
Even though you offer me your burnt offerings and your
   cereal offerings,
I will not accept them, and the peace offerings of your fatted
   beasts, I will not look upon.
Take away from me the noise of your songs;
to the melody of your harps I will not listen.
But let justice roll down like waters,
and righteousness like an ever-flowing stream (Am 5:21ff).

I cannot help feeling that God is still revealing his will to
us through Amos, the other prophets, and our own times. We
are in the midst of an age in Catholicism which is newly concerned with the liturgical format. We can read with amusement
about "the noise of your songs" and the "melody of your harps"
and easily find our modern substitutes. Whether we use pipe
organs, or electronic organs, or pianos, or guitars, or everything
or nothing, what difference does it make? It is all in vain unless
we worship God with justice and integrity.

I have heard the answer: "We are arriving at a sense of community. The fact that this is our own thing, the fact that we can
do our thing in the liturgy is what counts; it helps us individually
and as a community." So be it. I won't question for a moment
the psychological effect. My only question is, "To what avail?"
There are all sorts of communities; certainly the worshipers of
Baal formed a community and certainly the practice of cult
prostitution could have been argued as fostering togetherness.
The relevant point is this: Is today's liturgical concern with com-
munity-building equally concerned with building a community that
is Christian? I know that almost everyone who is trying to
change the liturgical format to foster community would answer
with an emphatic "Yes." Therefore it is necessary as always

to explain what one means by "Christian." In this particular
regard, I think that Karl Rahner remains unsurpassed in pointing
out that it is of prime importance for the Christian in his life —
liturgical and otherwise — to enter into the sacrificial disposition
of Christ at the Last Supper.[3]

In line with the thought of Amos, it seems to me that if a
particular liturgical format assists the believer to enter more
fully into communion with the mind and heart of Christ at the
Last Supper, then that format is basically valid. If it does not
contribute to that authentic communion or even impedes it, such
a liturgical format is in need of reform, no matter how enjoyable it may be. The question about today's liturgical formats is:
Do they assist the worshiper in entering into a real spirit of sacrifice, of giving of himself for the benefit of the other? Do they
have this same carry-over value in everyday life, even in such
areas as that of birth control?

I have mentioned three key elements in the prophetic message
which I think are relevant and valid for today: (1) the importance
of being mindful of the Covenant and of being faithful to it, (2)
the need and the difficulty of achieving authentic reform in one's
life, and (3) the realization that a change in liturgical format cannot be equated with this authentic reform. These three elements
have their parallel in the controversy over contraception and that
is why they have been included here.

(c) *Doctrine of the Remnant.* To speak of the doctrine of
the remnant in such a way as to imply that it may be applicable
once again in our time is to run the risk of being labeled a pessi-
mist. Yet in drawing a picture of the People of God, it seems
necessary to include this even though it takes on different colors
in historical perspective.

To the prophets the remnant was a sign of hope, a ray of
sunshine in an otherwise bleak and hopeless horizon. From a
people who departed from Yahweh and were punished by capti-

---

3. *Theological Investigations,* Vol. 3 (Baltimore, Md.: Helicon Press, 1967),
   p. 164.

vity, the Lord would gather up a remnant who would receive the fruit of the promise. Yahweh was still watching over them. He would not allow his people to fall into extinction.

What makes the doctrine of the remnant seem dark and pessimistic from our present point of view is the fact that today we have huge numbers in the visible Church. Certainly there is a restlessness not present in recent former years, but to those outside, the Catholic Church seems big and healthy. It is being called to reform, a call that has echoed in it before. Mention of the doctrine of the remnant would seem to imply some great purge in the offing, or some tremendous apostasy, a great rejection of the Church by the people or a great suppression on the part of the State. If we consider the Church as strong and healthy today then the doctrine of the remnant, the faithful few, may look pessimistic. On the other hand, if we regard the Church in its living human membership as weak or ailing, then the doctrine of the remnant carries with it that ray of sunshine and hope that Christ will not allow his people to suffer extinction though their numbers may be considerably reduced.

2. The People of God: New Covenant

The Covenant foretold by Jeremiah has come into being. Christ has fulfilled the Covenant of old and instituted a New Covenant which is meant to be written in the hearts of men and gladly accepted by each and all. No longer can it ever suffice to say that you are one of God's people, that you "know the Lord" if you perform the rituals. Now there must be an inner response to grace so that the externalization becomes an authentic representation of the whole person's acceptance of the Covenant with Christ.

In commenting on the doctrine of the People of God in the New Covenant, I am restricting myself to those aspects which I feel are relevant to the contraception controversy and perhaps can offer some balance to what has been written elsewhere in plenitude.

(a) *The Gospel for the Poor.* A few years ago it seemed that there was frequent reference in religious literature to the *anawim,* the Hebrew expression for God's poor, the little ones, the lowly. Today it is less prevalent.

Mary was the prime example of the *anawim.* Her *Magnificat* is a beautiful expression of what it meant to her to be one of God's poor.

> My soul magnifies the Lord, and my spirit rejoices in God my Savior, for he has regarded the low estate of his hand-maid . . . . He has shown strength with his arm, he has scattered the proud in the imagination of their hearts, he has put down the mighty from their thrones, and exalted those of low degree; he has filled the hungry with good things, and the rich he has sent empty away (Lk 1:46ff).

Because Mary was lowly, because she was not proud of heart, God did great things to her. When Luke tells us that she knew that all generations would call her blessed, we are likewise told that this was not Mary's work but God's. Mary looked to God completely for her salvation; she acknowledged completely her dependence upon him; she provides the model for the Christian who wants God to do great things in all believers.

Luke elaborates on this theme of the *anawim* in his account of the beatitudes which he balances with the prophetic woes.

> Blessed are you poor, for yours is the kingdom of God.
> Blessed are you that hunger now, for you shall be satisfied.
> Blessed are you that weep now, for you shall laugh.
> Blessed are you when men hate you, and when they exclude you and revile you, and cast out your name as evil, on ac-count of the Son of man. Rejoice in that day, and leap for joy, for behold, your reward is great in heaven; for so their fathers did to the prophets.
> But woe to you that are rich, for you have received your consolation.
> Woe to you that are full now, for you shall hunger.

Woe to you that laugh now, for you shall mourn and weep.
Woe to you, when all men speak well of you, for so their
fathers did to the false prophets (Lk 6:20-26).

This message forms a major theme in the gospel of Luke.
He relates the dangers of storing up wealth (12:13ff), the importance of realizing that "where your treasure is, there will your
heart be also" (12:34). The renunciation of possessions for
discipleship (14:28-33), the impossibility of being the slave of
both God and money (16:13), the parable of the rich man and
Lazarus who was poor (16:19ff), and the saying that "It is
easier for a camel to go through the eye of a needle than for a
rich man to enter the kingdom of God" (18:25) all permeate the
gospel according to Luke. It is no wonder that Harvey Cox said
of him that his gospel is "biased in favor of the poor."

So what's so great about being poor? Isn't this emphasis
on the theme of the danger of wealth awfully archaic and retro-
gressive? Don't we all know that what is really important is that
we have the *spirit* of poverty while doing all in our power to
put as large a gap as possible between actual poorness and ourselves?

It would seem to me that the gospel of Luke is telling us
that the man of means is in danger of putting his faith in his
money, or at least in his own ability to make money, to provide
for himself. In doing so, he becomes independent of God. He
no longer has the spirit of poverty which would prompt him to
put his trust in God, but he has become spiritually poor by putting his trust in himself .

The gospel theme of the danger of riches is most difficult
to talk about today in any public gathering. The chances are
that in any advertised meeting of Catholic laity you will have a
large proportion of Catholics who have spent large sums of money
for an education that has one main purpose: to enable him or
her to make good money. His whole education has been geared
to making him as independent as possible. It is one more aspect
of man's growing control of his environment, and every step
towards control of his environment carries with it the risk of

feeling independent of God. It is a risk that cannot be avoided, but one which must be recognized in order to be coped with.

Is the doctrine of the *anawim,* God's poor, relevant to the contraception controversy? It seems to me that the biblical theme of God's poor does indeed have a bearing on at least two of the popular arguments advanced on behalf of contraception. First of all, it would appear that there might be a contradiction between putting one's trust in God and doing all that one can to understand and control nature. Of course, such is not the case, for both are part of the biblical message. However, what can happen is that the effort to "subdue the earth" can become so much of a pre-occupation that trust in God is left behind in degrees so that eventually it is informally considered something only for the poor who cannot help themselves.

The sociological argument is, at least in the Northern part of the Western world where the contraception debate rings the loudest, largely a financial argument. "We can't afford to have another child." There is no denying the pressing financial condition of many people even in the Western world, but there is also no denying the financial prosperity of perhaps even more people in this same section of our globe. What bothers me is that the biblical doctrine of the People of God tells us that God's people are the poor, the *anawim.* On the other hand we have the new doctrine that a practice which may not advance the material prosperity of this particular family and may even lessen it can hardly be the will of God.

It seems to me that we are in danger of trying to have our cake and eat it too. If we want to bask in the realization that we are all God's people according to sound biblical doctrine, then it seems to me that we have to subject ourselves to a constant re-examination of conscience on how well we are accepting the fullness of the doctrine of God's people — including the fact that they are the *anawim.* Certainly it makes no sense at all, biblically speaking, to assert that since the doctrine of non-contraception may very well bring about economic hardship it cannot be the adequate expression of the will of God for our times. The realization that the People of God are characterized by being

God's little ones, his poor ones, his trusting ones would seem
rather to indicate that a practice (contraception) whose purpose
was to avoid the risk of the *anawim* would be contrary to the
will of God for our time and for any time — especially when the
alternative courses of action call for much reliance on help from
God and trust in his loving care.

(b) *Some New Testament Passages.* The prophetic tradition
of reminding the people of their greatness because of God's election and then recalling their corresponding obligations is replete
in the New Testament. The classic statement of being God's
people is found in 1 Peter 2:9ff.

> But you are a chosen race, a royal priesthood, a holy
> nation, God's own people, that you may declare the wonder-
> ful deeds of him who called you out of darkness into his
> marvelous light. Once you were no people but now you are
> God's people; once you had not received mercy but now you
> have received mercy.

Every phrase recalls the People of Israel, and now these
Gentile Christians are told that they are the New Israel, the
People of God. Along with this privilege of election, they have
the corresponding privilege and duty of proclaiming the work
of God: they are given a missionary mandate as a people,
not just as isolated individuals.

Paul's first letter to the Corinthians is a clear witness to
the pilgrim nature of this new People of God: "You are still
of the flesh. For while there is jealousy and strife among you,
are you not of the flesh, and behaving like ordinary men?" (1
Cor 3:3). He writes to bring the people to their senses (1 Cor
4:14) and shames them for condoning the incest of one of the
brethren (5:1ff). He reminds them that being the People of God
as a community is by no means any guarantee of their individual
holiness, for such was the case with Israel.

I want you to know, brethren, that our fathers were all

under the cloud, and all passed through the sea, and all were
baptized into Moses in the cloud and in the sea, and all ate
the same supernatural food and all drank the same supernatural drink. For they drank from the supernatural Rock
which followed them, and the Rock was Christ. Nevertheless
with most of them God was not pleased; for they were over-
thrown in the wilderness . . . .

Now these things happened to them as a warning, but
they were written down for our instruction, upon whom the
end of the ages has come. Therefore let any one who thinks
that he stands take heed lest he fall. No temptation has over-
taken you that is not common to man. God is faithful, and he
will not let you be tempted beyond your strength, but with
the temptation will also provide the way of escape, that you
may be able to endure it (1 Cor 10:1ff).

The followers of the Way were privileged, but this privilege
was no guarantee that they would find the way of the Spirit to
their liking or would follow it. They were subject just as their
spiritual forefathers to a double judgment: the judgment of man
for violating right order among men and the judgment of God both
for breaking the order of his creation and for violating the
Covenant.

There are today some extended treatments about the Church
as the People of God. Hans Küng illustrates at much greater
length and depth the stress implied in the calling to be God's
people.[4] My mention can be brief because I want to illustrate
just one thing in reference to the controversy on contraception. The evidence of both the Old Testament and the New
points to the reality that the popular instincts of the people have
no guarantee of being the work of the Spirit. On the contrary,
the biblical evidence is that the mass of the people regardless of
their educational level are in constant need of the prophetic
voice.

---

4. Hans Küng, *The Church* (New York: Sheed & Ward, 1968).

(c) *Consensus Fidelium: The Arian Question.* We have seen that the fact that great numbers of the People of God may see no wrong in contraception is no guarantee that this is the work of the Spirit. Paul tells us that most of the people under Moses were not pleasing to God and he uses this as a very pointed argument to humble the people at Corinth. Yet the phrase, *consensus fidelium,* the sense of the faithful, remains with us as one of the most powerful arguments advanced by the contraceptionists who persist in seeing in large numbers the evidence of the Holy Spirit. Thus it might be well to analyze briefly an historic situation in the Church which is used as a key element in today's controversy, the fidelity of the laity during the Arian heresy.

In July of 1859, John Henry Cardinal Newman published an essay titled "On Consulting the Faithful in Matters of Doctrine" in the *Rambler,* an English Catholic periodical. Its publication at a time when participation by the laity in the whole work of the Church was discouraged caused Newman to fall from favor as a middle-man between left and right in the Church of his day in England. The current emphasis on the laity as the People of God and the attempt to rid ourselves of an un-biblical caste system of "clerics" and "lay people" have revived interest in Newman's work.

Newman had written in the *Rambler* for May of that year that "in the preparation of a dogmatic definition, the faithful are consulted, as lately in the instance of the Immaculate Conception." [5] The statement drew theological objections and he answered them with the article "On Consulting the Faithful . . . ."

In this essay Newman explains how the witness of the faithful makes up for the absence of clear, authoritative teaching on the part of the magisterium and/or the theologians. He notes the thinking of a number of ancient Christian writers giving great weight to the consent of the faithful in matters of doctrinal controversy. Such consent and pious belief is really a reflection of what they have been taught by the "teaching Church."

5. John Coulson (ed.), *On Consulting the Faithful in Matters of Doctrine* (New York: Sheed & Ward, 1961).

The greater part of the essay is devoted to showing how the faithful were the primary voice of tradition during the sixty years following the Council of Nicea in 325. Newman notes case after case to illustrate his conviction that the great mass of the bishops were unfaithful to their commission, that general (non-ecumenical) councils erred, and that the Pope weakened and "communicated with the Arians and confirmed the sentence passed against Athanasius" (Coulson, p. 82). He notes that all of this went on at a time which was marked by the presence of a good number of men who would later be canonized as saints — "Athanasius, Hilary, the two Gregories, Basil, Chrysostom, Ambrose, Jerome, Augustine, and all of these saints bishops also, except one . . ." (p. 75).

Yet it was the faithful who remained the bulwark of orthodoxy, and he cites a number of cases to illustrate this. The faithful were subjected to all sorts of persecutions and by and large refused to enter the Arian communion although undoubtedly a number of them did. Their faith was that of the Council of Nicea and they would have no part with the theological tamperings and weakenings of the next sixty years.

Newman notes that an age similar to that of the Arian controversy may never come again. Speaking of his own times, exactly a hundred years ago, he could write in glowing terms, "As to the present, certainly, if there ever was an age which might dispense with the testimony of the faithful, and leave the maintenance of the truth to the pastors of the Church, it is the age in which we live. Never was the Episcopate of Christendom so devoted to the Holy See, so religious, so earnest in the discharge of its special duties, so little disposed to innovate, so superior to the temptation of theological sophistry — and perhaps this is the reason why the *consensus fidelium* has, in the minds of many, fallen into the background" (p. 103).

He concludes his essay by noting that "if ever there be an instance when they ought to be consulted, it is in the case of doctrines which bear directly upon devotional sentiments" (p. 104).

It seems to me that there are several points in Newman's explanation of the *consensus fidelium* that are relevant to the application of it to the contraception controversy.

(1) He uses as his examples only those cases which are a matter of dogmatic faith. He emphasizes that the sense of the faithful will be especially relevant in those matters of doctrine which have devotional connotations. He mentions in particular those dogmas concerned with the persons of Christ and his mother Mary.

(2) His "faithful" are those who reflect the tradition and who reject tampering with the tradition especially after it had been confirmed by the Council of Nicea. They are not the sophisticated, the theologians, the innovators; they are rather those who form a faithful reflection of what had been taught.

(3) The faithful by remaining faithful were subject to persecution. They had every material reason to go along with the times and the example of great numbers of priests and bishops who opted either for confusion or for denial of Nicea. The faithful had only spiritual, non-temporal reasons for remaining true to the doctrine of Nicea.

(4) The criteria for being counted among the faithful was simple: fidelity to the doctrine of Nicea.

By way of contrast, the situation today seems quite different from the one that Newman used to exemplify his theory on the witness of the faithful.

(1) While the Nicea controversy dealt with a matter of dogmatic faith, the present controversy deals with a matter of morals or lived doctrine. The former tended to be more of an "essential" question, i.e., it centered around the essence of Jesus Christ: what sort of a person was and is he? The question today

tends to be more of an existential question: how should I live
out the doctrine of Christian love in my marriage with regard
to the sexual act? Certainly the questions are related, but at least
today the immediacy of the two questions is felt differently. Perhaps we might say that the Nicene question is more important
while the contraception question is more urgent.

(2) While Newman's case is built upon a fidelity to official
doctrine by a Catholic people who seem to represent the humbler
classes, the advocates of contraception use the witness of the
most sophisticated section of the world to build a case for depart-
ing from the official doctrine. Newman's faithful were a reflection
of the action of the Spirit sustaining in the *anawim* his work which
had already been expressed through the official teaching of the
Catholic Church. The argument today takes the twist that through
the voice of a large segment of the Catholic laity, and perhaps
a majority of those who have been baptized as Christian, we
have a reflection of the Spirit working what he has been unable
to promulgate through the official teaching of the Catholic Church.
Newman painted a sorry picture of the many clerics who abandoned fidelity to Nicea or at least temporized, while today a
tabulation of clerics and others who oppose the official doctrine
is often looked upon with a sense of pride.

(3) The "conflict of interest" situation today is completely
reversed. Those who remained fully Catholic and loyal to Nicea
did so against their material interests. Today the same holds true
for those who accept as binding the traditional doctrine of the
Church on contraception as reaffirmed in *Humanae Vitae*. It
would seem that on the face of a parallel, the *consensus fidelium*
might better be taken from these. However, in their argument those
who advocate contraception make use of the voice of those who
stand to gain from a change in the doctrine. It seems somewhat
incongruous that, in our day when the masses, at the level of
public morality, strongly criticize the possibility of a conflict of
interest in public officials, Christian theologians should be basing

one of their chief arguments in favor of contraception on the judgment of people who are rather obviously involved in a conflict of interest. If it is thought that judgment may be impaired because of a conflict of interest at the level of the Supreme Court of the United States, we should ask ourselves to what extent judgment may be impaired because of a conflict of interest in matters of personal morality. The question is simply to what extent the voice of the laity who advocate contraception bears authentic witness to the Spirit of Christ and to what extent it partakes of the nature of a lobby for a vested interest. The fact that opposition to the teaching involves a conflict of interest does not add credibility to such opposition and certainly makes the case different from that which Newman described in the Arian conflict.

(4) A last and rather obvious difference between the situation described by Newman and the present is that in the Nicene period the *consensus fidelium* supported the official doctrine while today it is purported to oppose such official doctrine. Nor is it sufficient to say that the faithful of that time were adhering to a teaching that had been promulgated as *de fide,* as a defined dogma, while today we are treating of something taught with a lesser degree of formality and certitude. The present distinctions were not known then. Certainly most of the Catholics in the Nicene period did not regard the Council's teaching as a definition; rather they had fidelity to it simply because it was the clarified teaching of the Church. Then as now a case could be made for opposition. In retrospect today, we and Newman regard as the *consensus fidelium* the witness of the rank and file who accepted the Nicene clarification of the tradition in spite of the example set by much of the leadership of the Church.

The foregoing comments do not prove that those who advocate contraception are in error. However, I think I have shown that the argument from the *consensus fidelium* suggests that if we really have the *consensus fidelium* in those who practice and/or advocate contraception, then the Spirit and the faithful are acting in ways quite different from those described by Newman in the years following the Nicene statement of faith. If I have succeded in showing that the *consensus fidelium* is not at all the same as the gut reaction of many Catholics and is very much a two-edged sword in the present controversy, the analysis has been worthwhile.

3. The People of God: Today

The People of God of the Old Covenant present us with a picture of the Church of God always in need of reform in its humanity. The New Testament presents a similar view. The history of the Arian controversy shows that the faithful, the *anawim,* can be the steady vessel of election even when many a leader is opting for confusion or denial. What about the Church today? Do we find in it a clear picture that the people as a whole today are a visible manifestation of the workings of the Holy Spirit? Or is the scene so mixed or even so un-Christian that an argument from the thought and practice of a numerically significant section of this people is meaningless? What indications do we have that show a response or lack of response to the inspiration of the Holy Spirit?

(a) *The People and the Social Doctrine of the Church.* For over seventy-five years now, there has been an active promulgation of a social doctrine by the Church, beginning with *Rerum Novarum* of Leo XIII in 1891. This was followed after forty years by *Quadragesimo Anno* of Pius XI in 1931. Thirty years later, Pope John XXIII issued *Mater et Magistra* (1961), and then he issued the more political document that won world-wide acclaim, *Pacem in Terris* (1963). Pope Paul VI has continued this tradition with *Populorum Progressio* issued in 1967. How have these affected the Church as a whole? Specifically, how have the laity responded to this practical call of loving our neighbor?

Only the broadest sort of generalizations are possible in answer to such broad questions, and I will leave it to others either to refute my general answers or to back them up with detailed research. However, I expect very little criticism of the following comments.

(1) The Church as a whole has not become a sign of love and concern for others. A chronicler of the twentieth-century struggle for the rights of the workingman would not include the efforts of the mass of Catholic laity or clergy on behalf of the oppressed except when *they* were the oppressed. We can point to some wonderful exceptions to this general rule — the self-sacrificing individual missionaries, Dorothy Day, and a few others like her — but we will search in vain for any long tradition of the laity accepting the social doctrine of the Church and trying to apply it in the world.

Much of this can be explained in North America by the fact that prior to World War II the Catholic population was numerically and politically insignificant in terms of the power it wielded. Many Catholics were recent immigrants and even the second generation of imigrants found themselves disadvantaged economically and educationally.

However, in our own era the reaction of the laity as a whole to the doctrine of social justice has been mixed, to say the least. The reaction to the racial problem by Catholics has found a few leading the way and a great many more emphatically opposed to anything more than paper equality. Frequently, those white Catholics in the vanguard of the black civil rights movement had nothing to lose economically while those opposed feared economic loss.

(2) The Church as a whole in our times has not been noted for its sense of community. The social doctrine promulgated by the Church stresses both the dignity of the individual person and the community of man. It teaches the obligation of those who have a sufficient amount of this world's goods to share gene-rously with those who do not. Yet the statistics on how the affluent section of the Church helps the poor Church are sorry indeed. To be sure, much of this can be explained away by the fact that the primary form of giving, the Sunday contribution,

gives distribution control to clerics who too frequently have had a narrow sense of their responsibility. Yet, the special collections for the missions and the missioners own begging has pitiful per-household results.

(3) Those Catholics who have stood to lose economically by a more just distribution of wealth and a more just social order have generally ignored or opposed the social doctrine of the Church. Latin America is a classic example. Both rich and poor are Catholics. The educated are Catholic. Yet Catholic Latin America is now the scene of the gravest social evils. For seventy-eight years the social doctrine of the Church has been pointedly ignored by those who had the physical freedom to put them into effect. To be sure, the social doctrine has never been taught with the theological note of infallibility; and even if it were, it would still remain a matter of individual conscience to accept and apply it. However, the way in which affluent Catholics have formed and followed their consciences in this matter raises some very serious questions about the effort they put into searching after the truth.

(4) The reaction of affluent Catholicism to *Populorum Progressio* (1967) and *Humanae Vitae* (1968) can be read as indicating that the People of God are motivated much more by self-interest than by self-giving. The Churches of the poor have acclaimed *Populorum Progressio* and have said relatively little about *Humanae Vitae*. I remember a letter to the editor in the summer of 1968 in which the writer told of an international conference. Delegates from Europe and North America were upset by *Humanae Vitae;* delegates from the underdeveloped countries were almost unconcerned. They said they didn't fear exploitation from Rome anywhere near as much as economic exploitation from Europe and North America.

(5) Despite the tradition of ignoring or opposing the social doctrine of the magisterium by the People of God who would have

something to lose by practicing it, dialoging Catholics still point to this social doctrine with great pride. It remains on the documentary level a sign that Popes at least were interested in teaching about the dignity and brotherhood of man. It will remain for historians a sign of at least verbal effort at reform in a Church always in need of reform.

My comments on the People of God with regard to the papal social doctrine have been negative and pessimistic. Perhaps somebody will refute them; I hope so, but I doubt it. Certainly, there have been glorious exceptions, but by and large self-interest seems to have dominated, love has been cast out by fear, and the overall response of the People of God has been no different from that of the "world."

(b) *"Post-Christianity."* Another difficulty in accepting the testimony of large numbers of Christians about the permissibility of contraception is that these Christians are living in an age which is being called "post-Christian." Presumably, this means that the spirit of the day is not that of the Spirit of God, that extreme empiricism has crowded out faith, and that the value system of Christ is either discounted or accepted piecemeal — insofar as it coincides with other philosophies about man but devoid of its constant reference to heaven and the Father.

In some formerly "Catholic areas" churches are known for the absence of men. In the United States some recent statistics show that total Church membership (Protestant and Catholic) is up while total attendance is down, suggesting that more and more people are going to church less and less.

The question is, in an era being called post-Christian by its contemporary theologians, how do we tell the *real* Christians from the *apparent ones?* I have no answer but only a suggestion from biblical history. The biblical doctrine of the People of God would indicate that when the people become indistinguishable from the men of the world, taken in a pejorative sense, then perhaps we are at a time when the doctrine of the remnant will again give us hope. However the doctrine of the remnant suggests small numbers, not large.

Contraception has certainly been bought by that section of the world called post-Christian. It has been accepted by the formally non-religious as well as by that segment bearing the name of Christian. It has been attempted by man for about five thousand years and now seems to be reaching a state of scientific perfection. Our question is whether its use helps the Christian to attain that moral perfection to which Christ is calling him.

The advocates of contraception point to the numbers of Protestants and Catholics who see nothing wrong and lots of good in contraception as a sign that the Spirit of God is speaking through them to the magisterium which must listen and change. My remarks about post-Christianity have been intended only to show the danger of assuming that large numbers indicate the work of the Holy Spirit. The witness of these Christians must be balanced by the fact that (1) they are witnessing to something in perfect accord with the spirit of the day; (2) the spirit of the day is labelled post-Christian by many religious writers; (3) the doctrines of the remnant and the *anawim* should make us wary of the testimony of large numbers about a matter that is to their material benefit and requires no faith to live it.

(c) *The Virtue of Chastity.* A third question that deserves our attention is, "Are Christian people today developing the virtue of chastity?" There is no way that I can point to one person or another and say, "That person has this virtue; that one doesn't." We'll have to leave the individual judgments to God. There are, however, some public indications that are at least thought provoking although admittedly not conclusive. Harvey Cox has written some pages that are particularly relevant to our effort to judge whether Christian peoples today are developing the virtue of chastity, and I think it best to quote rather liberally.[6]

Remember also that dating (and with it various types of petting) now reaches down to the sixth grade. Youngsters

---

6. Harvey Cox, *The Secular City* (New York: Macmillan, 1965), pp. 206-207.

are thus exposed for a longer period and much more intensely to the mutual exploitation of erogenous regions which is the American courtship pattern. The only advice they get is, "Don't go too far," and it is usually the girl who is expected to draw the line.

By the time a girl who begins petting at thirteen has reached marriageable age, she has drawn an awful lot of lines. If she is especially impressed with her religious duty to avoid sexual intercourse, she will probably have mastered, by twenty-one, all the stratagems for achieving a kind of sexual climax while simultaneously preventing herself and her partner from crossing the sacrosanct line.

Cox then asks why young people do not hear the Christian sexual ethic as "evangelical," as good news. He believes it has been dissolved into a myth, frozen into a Law. He then proceeds to free it from the myth.

Both the romantic ideal and the identification of intercourse with coitus are cultural accretions that have been coalesced with the rule of premarital chastity . . . .

The ideal of romantic love is the most obvious mythical excrescence. It leads often to the belief, especially among girls, that certain forms of intimacy become progressively less objectionable the more you love the boy . . . Among adolescents of all ages, *love* has come to mean nothing more than a vague emotional glow.[7]

Obviously, one does not have to agree with Cox's solutions in order to agree with his analysis of the problem. He then proceeds to zero in on what I believe is one of the firmest indications that our Christian people are not really developing the virtue of chastity.

A more stubborn and deceptive segment of folklore that has been equated with the doctrine of premarital chastity is one

7. *Ibid.*, pp. 208-209.

that is rarely discussed openly: the curious presumption that a person who has not experienced coital intercourse remains a virgin — no matter what else he or she has done. This popular piece of legerdemain explains in part the discovery by Kinsey that, although the incidence of premarital intercourse among women has merely mounted steadily, premarital petting of all varieties has skyrocketed.

Kinsey's finding could be substantiated by the most casual observer of the American college scene. The number of students who do not pet at all is negligible. An increasing number regularly carry their necking to the point of heavy sex play and orgasm. A pert young graduate of a denominational college assured me recently that although she had necked to orgasm every week-end for two years, she had never "gone all the way." Her premarital chastity was intact.

Or was it? Only, I submit, by the most technical definition of what is meant by preserving virginity. True, some writers actually advocate such noncoital orgasm as the safest way for unmarried people to achieve sexual climax. However distasteful this idea may seem to some, it is extremely important to realize that the Church's traditional teaching actually functions in such a fashion as to give considerable support to this view.

The ideal of premarital chastity is generally understood to mean that, although necking is somewhat questionable, the fragile gem of virginity remains intact so long as coitus is avoided. This myth has helped open the floodgate to a tidal wave of noncoital promiscuity." [8]

If the above quotation provides a fair estimate of the premarital patterns for the American people as a whole, then there is ample reason to doubt that our Christian people are developing the virtue of chastity. Perhaps certain religious groups are above this average, perhaps Catholics were not interviewed in sufficient numbers by Kinsey. However, if the picture is valid

8. *Ibid.*, pp. 210-211.

and if it applies to Christians as well as to non-Christians, then we can trace the following development of a typical couple.

In our day and age, even before the onset of puberty, social pressures are being used to break down the natural reserve that most young people have to members of the opposite sex. At the onslaught of puberty with all its strong drives, social pressures multiply the biological drives. To prove himself, the boy is practically forced to do something to some girl that will show that he's not pure, not sissy. Similar pressures are brought to bear on many girls. Then as our young boy and girl advance from the pressures of the peer group to an area of greater self assertion, they find that sexual permissiveness provides a way of showing your special liking for one another. Frequently a spiraling round of affective behavior is set in motion. At first a goodnight kiss communicates their liking. Then just a little sitting together and a few kisses. Then empassioned embraces and finally the use of each other's bodies for purely sexual ends. The petting has but one or two purposes: (1) either to lead to a form of mutual masturbation in which at least one or perhaps both seek non-coital orgasm, or (2) to lead to sexual intercourse.

By the time our young man and young woman are ready to marry they have very likely developed sexual habits which are designed to cope with sexual tension only through the seeking of sexual relief in orgasm. If they are Christian, they cloak all this under the myth that pre-marital chastity is synonymous with non-coitus.

It should be obvious to anyone that Christian people who form this sort of view of chastity are scarcely going to see anything wrong with contraception. For them for some years, sex has become a means of personal expression, of regular practice, and of regular relief. If there was no one available from the opposite sex, masturbation provided an easy form of getting rid of the problem; for they had long been told that the only thing wrong about masturbation was that it showed a lack of maturity. The virtue of chastity, a power that controls the sex drive to put it at the service of authentic love according to one's state in life, simply has not been developed. The preservation of virginity in the technical sense of non-coitus, where done at all, is due much less to the development of the virtue of chastity than to a very practical form of prudence. Fear, not love, has been the motive.

If spouses have not individually developed the virtue of chastity during their pre-marital years, the demands of marital chastity taught by the magisterium are going to seem unreasonable and unbearable. If these people have thought that by engaging in all sorts of deliberately stimulating sexual activity in their dating years they were behaving in a Christian manner, then the doctrine of non-contraception with its corollary of self-control is bound to seem un-Christian to them.

Thus when we read that Protestants and many Catholics see nothing wrong with contraception, we should be wary of attributing this witness to the Holy Spirit. We need to know first of all whether these are the voices of persons who have really developed the virtue of chastity or whether they are themselves in need of reform and renewal. The witness of Kinsey and Cox would indicate that non-coital promiscuity is by no means confined to the non-baptized and that the heavy petting habits of unchastity are to be found on all campuses, religious and secular.

(d) *Sociology and Morality.* For the Christian and the Jew, it would seem quite obvious that what "the nations," the people of the world are doing would not be a criteria for morality. The prophets of old chastized the people of the Old Covenant for slipping into the ways of their neighbors. For the people of the New Covenant, the norm is Christ, the way is the life of the Spirit, not that of the self-interested flesh.

Yet in the entire sexual revolution which has taken place in this century, the sociological survey seems to be replacing the gospel. For many the criteria is the "average" behavior of mankind. If everybody's doing it, it can't be too bad; in fact, it must be O.K.

The contraception controversy has seen repeated use of sociology as a subtle substitute for determining the norm. The sociological survey has indicated that Protestants (with some exceptions) and Jews (and the completely secular irreligious, too) see nothing wrong with contraception. Then the surveys showed that a large proportion of Long Island Catholic housewives used some form of birth control; then other surveys showed a certain Catholic acceptance of the Pill, and then of other contraceptives. The issuance of *Humanae Vitae* brought a regular weekly tally of the number of priests who disagreed with the Pope, and we can expect rapid surveys for years to come.

This amounts to an argument from authority, the authority of the masses. "How can the masses be wrong?" it asks. I can only respond that the biblical evidence shows us that the masses have been wrong before and have stood in urgent need of God's word to which all men must render obedience in faith if they are to be saved. The norm is Christ; we have no guarantee whatsoever that the voice of the people, be they Jewish, Protestant, Catholic or pagan, provides us with the voice of the Spirit.

(e) *The Need for the Prophetic Voice.* Scripture shows us the need of God's people for the prophetic voice. Moses was raised up to lead the people out of the slavery of Egypt and through the confusion and trials of the wilderness. The prophets of the eighth and sixth centuries before Christ called the people to leave a new type of slavery, one which they had made for themselves out of their own material self-interest. The people of the new Christian churches were also the beneficiaries of some distinctive prophets — Peter, Paul and others. Once again, the people proved themselves in need of a prophetic reminder to be faithful to the Covenant in which they had been raised to the life and the way of the Spirit.

The word of Scripture remains normative for the people of every age. Of itself it provides God's constant call to communal and individual *metanoia,* that change of heart so necessary to live out the gospel. So important is the word of Scripture that it would seem that there would be no further need for the prophetic word. Christ, the fullness of the prophets, has come and has spoken. He has structured a living Church so that the Word of God in Scripture could be transmitted in a living way to all

generations. To his Church as a whole, he entrusted the mission
of being his voice to all the nations: "You are God's people . . .
to proclaim his wonderful work . . ." (1 Pet 2:9ff).

The history of the Church has shown that the Spirit has
raised up men and women from time to time in a very prophetic
role, e.g., Athanasius, Catherine of Siena, Francis of Assisi,
Savanarola, and other great figures in the life of the Church. It
was their responsibility to call for a reform, a renewal, a return
to the Covenant of the Lord.

Today, I doubt that many would question the fact that the
People of God are in need of a strong and clear prophetic voice.
Too many problems beset the Church to allow complacency in
any area of her life. But where is that voice to be found? Will
God raise up some person who will be recognized by all or by
many as some sort of a prophetic figure? Even if this did happen,
the odds are that he or she wouldn't be recognized as such until
later generations, so the present age would still be confused —
perhaps even more so by an additional debate over personalities.

I would like to submit that one of the charismatic functions
of the Petrine office is to be the steadying, prophetic voice for
the entire People of God. I realize full well that the Old Testament
prophets of the eighth and sixth centuries before Christ were
outside the official structure, and the prophetic figures I have
mentioned from the history of the Catholic Church have likewise
been outside them. It would seem at first that there is almost
a contrariness, if not a contradiction, between being used by the
Spirit as a prophetic voice and being a member of the hierarchy.
However, wouldn't we be thinking in excessively narrow categories
to assume that such a contrariness was inevitable or the norm?

Scripture shows us in a very clear fashion that Christ joined
in Peter both the structural role of headship and the role of
prophet, spokesman for the Lord. Peter is the Lord's prophet
on the day of Pentecost and on the succeeding days in the *Acts*.
He is also the Lord's prophet in admitting the first Gentile, Cor-
nelius, into the Church. The fact that he is not the only prophetic
voice certainly proves that this charism is by no means exclusive;
but the fact that he fulfills both the leadership and prophetic roles

also proves that in the Petrine office the two have been combined.

The definition of papal infallibility by Vatican I teaches us that under some very specific conditions we can have the certainty of divinely illuminated faith that the Petrine office is exercising its prophetic role as a teacher of the truth. Since the formulation of that dogma such conditions have been met only twice: in the definitions of the Marian dogmas of the Immaculate Conception and the Assumption. The question on people's minds today concerns the role of the Petrine office in the exercise of the ordinary magisterium. Is the apparent loneliness of the Pope on the birth control question the loneliness of the prophet of God? Is the rejection of his call to a high and difficult way of marital life the rejection usually accorded to the prophets of old?

I would like to offer three reasons why I think that Pope Paul VI is being used in a prophetic role. First of all, according to the theory of sex presented in Section III, Paul is calling the people to live up to the demands of the Covenant — the marriage Covenant which sacramentalizes the Covenant of Christ and his Church. If this is in fact what he is doing, he is firmly in the tradition of the classical prophets whose primary mission was to call the people back to the living of the Covenant. Secondly, he is obviously asking the people to be faithful to the tradition. This again was a prime function of the prophet. Thirdly, the popes of recent years have been fulfilling, in my opinion, a genuine prophetic role in the promulgation of the social gospel. They have likewise been constant in their call to marital chastity. I realize that none of these three reasons *proves* anything about the truth of *Humanae Vitae*; I offer them only as reasons that incline me to believe that it is more likely than not that the prophetic role of Peter is being presently exercised in the Petrine office by Paul.

* * *

This chapter has been an analysis of the appeal to the voice of the People of God. The appeal raises the question about where we can find the voice of the Spirit in the controversy over contraception. The biblical evidence shows us that we should not be surprised in the least if, in a matter of morality closely tied in with one's material interests, the voice of the People should err. We should not be surprised if the bearer of the voice of the Spirit, the prophetic figure for our times, seems alienated from the people to whom he speaks; for such was the case with the prophets of old. It may very well be that this chapter has been one-sided. I would not want to try to defend myself from that criticism. There is only so much space, and my purpose has been not to present an entire theology of the People of God but only to balance some current assumptions.

It is common to read that some priest, bishop, or cardinal has said that married people are better experts on marriage than the Pope. I would hope that I have succeeded in showing that such a statement, taken just as it stands, is meaningless. A statement like that is no more meaningful than these: "Employers are the experts on the moral aspects of the employment relationship." "The police are the experts on human rights." "Bishops and religious superiors are the experts on religious obedience." "The Curia are the experts on Church administration." "Pastors are the experts on parish matters." All of these statements border on the absurd because they assume that the people named have developed the virtues necessary for the Christian fulfillment of their respective duties. Each of these statements is widely denied because it has become apparent that too often the people who hold the various positions have a warped and one-sided view of reality; too often they look at the matter through eye-glasses of self-interest and self-preservation in office.

Saying that married people are better experts on marriage than the Pope is equally as meaningless as these other statements. It assumes that these married people have developed the necessary virtues, and attitudes — chastity, spiritual prudence, trust, the spirit of poverty, and the obedience of faith. It makes this assumption in the face of widespread evidence that the virtue of chastity is generally undeveloped and that materialism affects Christian peoples no less than non-Christian, that the specifically

"Christianized" world is today the source of economic exploitation of the undeveloped nations, and that it is also labelled "post-Christian" by its own theologians. There is ample evidence suggesting that the spirit of the age is not that of the Holy Spirit and that we Christians, in our sexual lives as well as in all other areas of life, stand in need of a strong prophetic voice calling us back to a renewed living of the Covenant in which we can be saved.

The sacrament of Matrimony does not bring with it the virtue of chastity in any automatic form. If we were not chaste before marriage, it is very likely that we will experience considerable difficulty with authentic norms of Christian chastity within marriage. If I have succeeded in leading some married couples to examine themselves seriously in this matter, I would suggest that a step has been taken in the right direction.

THEOLOGICAL AND PHILOSOPHICAL ASPECTS OF THE CONTROVERSY

Chapter Four

A CRITIQUE OF THE CONTRACEPTIVE ARGUMENTS

It is impossible in less than several volumes to offer a critique of all the contraceptive theology that has been written or popularized in the last half dozen years, say since the beginning of Vatican II (October, 1962). However, as one who has tried to keep somewhat abreast of the major currents of thought, I think I have assimilated certain main lines of argumentation, and it is these that I hope to criticize. Some of them would be uttered by no responsible theologian today; yet in this controversy they have become part of the popular arsenal and need to be examined even if only very briefly.

1. The Argument from Science

This argument is typically phrased along these lines. Until recently man has not known about efficient means of contraception. Now new medical knowledge has given us extremely efficient ways of contraception, especially the Pill. God gave man a brain to use it to control nature. Therefore God permits contraception, and intelligent man should use the means most efficient for him. The worth of the argument is easily seen by substituting another value. "Until recently man has not known about efficient means of mass killing. Now new scientific knowledge has given us extremely efficient ways of mass killing, especially the hydrogen bomb. God gave man a brain to use it to control nature. Therefore God permits mass killing and intelligent man should use the means most efficient for him — in this case the H-bomb." No one, I hope, would subscribe to the "logic" of the second argument. Everybody, I hope, would say that the argument says nothing about the morality of mass killing and that the *use* of our new scientific knowledge has to be evaluated according to moral principles. The fact that we know *how* to do something, even if it has taken the work of geniuses to discover it, does not mean that it is *good* to do it. And that is equally true about contraception, the use of the Pill or any other device. Knowledge of newer and more efficient means of contraception, even though the work of brilliant scientists, is of itself no indication that it is good to practice contraception, either in the older forms such as Onan's withdrawal before ejaculation or the newer forms such as the Pill. The argument from science is simply no argument.

2.   A New Concept of Man

Somewhat related to the argument from science, the theory of a new concept of man stresses man's dynamism. Man is no longer content to look upon nature as a static thing of which he is the passive subject. Rather, he seeks to control nature. Now that he knows more about fertility it is natural for him to control it so that he can be true to his role as a dynamic, self-determining being. He may and should therefore use whatever scientific means he can to control the fertility aspect of nature.

It is true that modern man is probably considerably more aware, self-consciously aware, of being dynamic and self-determining than previous generations have been. It is equally true that man has always been dynamic, he always sought to "control nature" in one way or another. Ancient civilizations had well-planned and well-functioning irrigation systems. Probably every war that was ever fought was a result of somebody's dissatisfaction with the "natural" boundaries of his tribe or kingdom. The building of boats, (and how primitive is that?) is evidence of man's desire to master the "natural" boundary of water.

Change has been noted as a fact of life ever since Heraclitus immortalized it in his teaching that the only constant is change. What is new about change today is that it is (1) much more rapid than ever before, (2) more self-consciously sought by agents of change, (3) found influencing almost every facet of life. Yet the emphasis on man's self-conscious dynamism leaves unexplained that which remains the same. Why is it that I can read the Old Testament and relate to the people there? Why is it that I can read the plays and the epics of the ancient Greeks and relate to them? Is it not because at the same time that man is by nature dynamic he is also by that same nature static?

I can hear the critics now. "Kippley has a static concept of nature, and if you can abide anyone so archaic . . . etc." My position is that the truth lies in a philosophy of "both . . . and." Man is unchanging in some ways and changing in others. I believe that man is basically unchanging with regard to his interpersonal relationships but that he is changing with regard to his self-conscious awareness of those relationships. Man has always been a community being, has always known that he had certain rights and that others had certain rights. He has had to grow — evolve, if you please — into a conscious understanding that all men are one community, that the community exists for the sake of the individual person, etc. The conflict with communism today shows the difficulty with which this latter consciousness is evolving.

The argument from a new concept of man says nothing at all about the morality of contraception. It is one-sided in its emphasis on man's self-determining dynamism, and even if this were the full truth, it still would not be a *reason* for contraception. At the best it would be a reason for investigating further whether married sexual intercourse is a proper subject for willful interference.

3. The Argument from Sociology

The sociological argument might well be called the argument from present difficulties. This line of thought reminds us that in the immediate past we were more of an agrarian culture where children were an economic asset. Perhaps so, but this says nothing at all about the Irish rural economy in which a large family was certainly no economic asset, nor does it say anything about the history of civilization which is basically a history of the cities. It seems to me that this places too much emphasis on what has happened in North America during the last forty or fifty years. After the frontiers were settled, machinery came in, and people began migrating to urban centers. If the majority of people lived on farms, there have always been a great number of people who lived in the cities where large families have never been an economic asset.

The sociological thought forcefully reminds us of the population expansion. It tends to center on global population, while individual married couples tend to center on the population within their own family. The sociological argument reminds us also of the desirability of higher education for all and the expense of this for the large family. We cannot help but become aware of the difficulties for both nations and individual families.

The argument seems to run something like this: 1. Today there are tremendous, even unprecedented sociological difficulties in our world. 2. The economy of the rich nations seems geared for a family of not over three children. The economy of the poor nations leads many to starvation. 3. Man has a duty to better his whole world. He has created part of the problem by lowering the natural death rate. 4. He has the physical power to limit population through contraception. 5. Therefore it is permissible, even perhaps mandatory, to practice contraception in the present sociological circumstances.

The argument is extremely attractive. I think that every statement up to the "therefore" conclusion is true. The problem is that the conclusion is by no means contained in the preceding statements. The argument assumes what needs to be proved, i.e., that contraception is in itself a morally permissible way of expressing married love. This can be illustrated simply by substituting other means in the statement 4. "He has the physical power to limit population through —————." Put in contraception, genocide, infanticide, abortion, the destruction of the incurably sick, the killing of the old, the sterilization of non-contraceptive parents, and you can see that what remains to be proved is that anyone of these is morally acceptable. That is, the existence of external pressures is no sure sign at all that either contraception or any other method of population control is morally permissible. The existence of the external pressures is, of course, a sure sign that we should take a very close look at what is involved in each one of these and other physically possible methods.

I am quite willing to grant that contraception is a much lesser evil than any of the other methods of population control mentioned above. It alone does not violate the rights of a third person. However, what concerns me is that the sociological argument, first used to justify contraception, is now being used to justify abortion, and it is being used in this way by spokesmen for Christian Churches. What has happened, I fear, is that the method of reasoning from external difficulty has led too many to stop asking themselves, "What is it that I am doing right now, regardless of my intention. Am I invalidating an act of love? Am I killing a person who has just as much right to live as I do?" This argument or line of reasoning still avoids the issue of what is involved in contraception. It seems to assure that it is an indifferent biologism whose moral character is ascertained solely by reference to the external economic and other sociological circumstances. Thus it assumes what needs to be proved; it provides at the best a very good reason to more closely examine the morality of contraception itself.

4.   The Love Union

The most potent of the arguments for contraception centers around the affective love that can be expressed in sexual intercourse.

Married couples witness to the fact that they have various needs — affective, psychological, physiological — which are satisfied through the expression of their affection and love in the sexual union. Married couples testify to the tension that occurs when they wish to have relations and yet are fearful of pregnancy. They want to express their love in the sexual union, and it seems so natural to do so that it seems unnatural to refrain. It is generally agreed that when there are physical indications that the couple should refrain from sexual intercourse, it would not be loving for the husband or the wife to insist upon "making love." Here there seems to be an understanding that the processes of "nature" sometimes exclude doing what comes naturally in the way of affective love. Still, these are regarded as the exceptions which only serve to point up the rule that "normal" married behavior between two people who love each other is to have relations when they feel like it.

In the earlier stages of the controversy it seemed to be held that the married sexual union was an expression of married *agapé,* a self-giving love. As it was pointed out that contraception was reservation, that there could not be a complete self-giving in contraceptive intercourse, we heard that man was never capable of complete self-giving at any time, that he always loved with reservation. Then we began to see that the uniquely Christian word for love, *agapé,* was dropped by some in favor of *eros,* and the values of erotic love were worthy to be sought or enjoyed for their own sake; these too were the works of God. Puritanism has been left behind.

There is no use denying that the personalist, affective, and erotic values of sex have long been repressed in the *imprimatur* writings of Catholics. There is no denying that the emphasis on the procreative aspects of sex as "primary" had the effect of putting the "secondary" aspects of marriage in an entirely inferior position. It was as if *both* could not be maintained as purposes or values within marriage, as if to admit both would exclude one or the other. This still remains a valid question: can people psychologically hold both the procreative and unitive aspects in a creative tension, or will they not in fact actually deny one in their emphasis of the other? I think that a much stronger historical case can be made for the latter, but I believe that the truth lies in keeping both elements in a creative tension. Barrels of ink have described the ecclesiastical repression of the personalist, affective, erotic values, so no space has to be devoted to that here. However, has not the current contraceptive mentality done the same thing to the procreative values?

The proponents of contraception who strive to give due credit to the procreative aspects of the sexual union while emphasizing the unitive aspects sometimes give the impression that the pro-creative aspects may be denied for a time because the marriage is basically open to life. Without saying it in so many words, they infer that the marriage is basically open to life because most of the time the procreative and unitive aspects of the marital union are not positively separated. If this is what they mean by being basically open to life, I fear they have not taken a good reading on what is going on in the average contraceptive marriage. Young people are being urged not to have over two children, three at the maximum. If a couple decides upon this course and fall into a somewhat average pattern of sexual relations about two or three times a week, over the course of their fertile years they will have allowed less than ten percent of their sexual acts to be open to the possibility of procreation. Where over ninety percent of marital sex acts contraceptively separate the unitive and procreative aspects of marriage, is it realistic to say that such a marriage is basically open to life? Would it not be more realistic to admit that such marriages represent a *de facto* denial of the procreative values of sex?

Furthermore, I have a great difficulty in seeing how the love union approach can make an adequate distinction between casual, pre-marital, marital, and extra-marital affections. If the new sin is denial of one's affective love, on what philosophical grounds can we ask young lovers to deny themselves? Scripture is of only limited help, for it can be interpreted into meaninglessness, and everybody knows that the Church has defined only a half dozen or so passages of Scripture. Ethicians counsel against ex-ploiting each other. Others bring in a Kantian motive: consider that your actions are the norm for everybody else. But what if a young couple, well read in the philosophy of the love union, come to their parents and say that they are simply so fond of each other, so full of love, that full sexual expression seems natural, that they are not exploiting each other, that they hope every young couple feels the same way, and that they don't feel that a fundamentalist interpretation of Scripture is relevant to their case? What if they should then ask, "If denial of strong affective love is bad for you, why isn't it bad for us too?" What do the parents of the love-union contraceptive mentality answer? I give an answer based on the marriage covenant in a later chapter, but on the basis of affective love, I am at a loss. The "wait and it will be more meaningful" answer only brings the question, "Why can't married people wait ten days or two weeks? You're asking me to wait for years." If spontaneity is so important in married life, why isn't it equally valid among the unmarried whose psychological needs for affection may be considerably greater than those of a happily married couple? This application of the principle to an area of moral life outside of marital contraception seems logical enough. It also carries the seed of moral chaos, and it illustrates the danger of some of the principles used to solve the contraception question.

Nor is it of any value for the advocates of marital contraception to state that sex out of marriage is illicit and that they are adamantly opposed to casual, premarital, and extramarital sex. Their argument from their own authority is rather gratuitous. They must be able to explain *why* the principle of the affective love-union may not be applied universally wherever there is a strong affective love that desires to express itself in the sexual union.

In summary, the argument from the affective love-union admirably reflects the feelings of many married couples. At the same time it fails to distinguish adequately between married and unmarried love. It also fails to hold a real balance between the procreative and affective values in marriage. It fails to relate adequately the Christian *agapé*, self-giving love with the seemingly universal tendency to *eros*, pleasurable love.

5.   The Principle of the Total Human Act

I have commented on several of the chief lines of argumentation that seem to be popular today — the emphases on our new
scientific knowledge, a new understanding of man, the sociological
difficulties and the personal love-union. I would characterize these
as "new subject matter" approaches to the problem. They seem
to say, "Look at this. This has changed, this is new, this is different,
this is better. Our non-contraceptive tradition was formed before
we had these new insights. The traditional insights have been
replaced. Therefore contraception is good or at least permissible."
Other approaches are based more on principle rather than on
subject matter, and I will try to offer a critique of three of these.

We have all learned that it is false to say that the end justifies
the means. This has been so ingrained in most of us that even
the most radical of the new Catholic theologians feel uneasy about
flatly contradicting it. Thus I cannot remember having seen in print
yet the statement that we were wrong before, but now we know
that the end does justify the means. Another way of stating the
principle is to say that intention does not justify an action which
is morally wrong in the objective order. Likewise the theologians
of the new morality have not yet, to my knowledge, made the
good intention the sole criteria of morality although everyone recognizes that an ignorant good intention can remove an otherwise
evil act from the realm of subjective sin and guilt.

However, despite the verbal repetition that morality does
not consist just in good intentions, there is a way of explaining
our actions which, in my opinion, does in fact make morality
(and not just culpability) dependent solely upon the intention
while proclaiming all the while that it does not. For lack of a
better term, I will label this way of reasoning "the principle of
the total human act." [1] In using this term, I am combining what

---

1. For persuasive descriptions of this, see W. H. Van der Marck, O.P.,
   Love and Fertility (London: Sheed & Ward, 1965), and *Toward a
   Christian Ethic* (Paramus, N.J.: Paulist/Newman Press, 1967).

is sometimes called "the principle of totality" with the theory of the truly human act. In my opinion, the two are inseparably linked.

This principle says that it is misleading to speak of "end" and "means" because to do so separates an inseparably unified human act. The customary way of speaking looks at the "means" as the material physical act and the "end" as the motive of the actor. It divides into neat but unrealistic categories a unified action of a person. There is no simple material substratum which is made good or bad by the "end." There is only the human act which is matter-spirit in particular circumstances and has to be evaluated as a totality, not just as a physical thing. W. Van der Marck, O.P., uses the term intersubjectivity in his effort to emphasize the importance of the uniquely human aspect of a truly human action: the fact that it is not just a material act but is being done by a free human person who is doing this material thing as part of the larger human act of acting with a purpose.

Examples abound. Take this knife held by this hand slitting this skin. What's going on? Much more than just skin-slitting. It can be a medical operation by a skilled surgeon, torture, murder, etc. Or again, suppose that the knife is being thrust into this person in such a way as to end his life. What is the human value of the act? Is it murder or self-defense or capital punishment? The anatomical description does not do justice to the action as a truly human act. So far, no problem.

This line of reasoning then points to the history of Catholic moral theology as having been excessively materialistic and devisive of the total human act. Here a favored example is the development of the doctrine concerning human transplants. When the question first arose, primarily after World War II, the moralists looked upon it as a mutilation (bad) even if done to help another (good). The end was seen as good but the means was bad. Therefore, it was forbidden. At the same time, it became apparent to many that excessive attention paid to anatomical integrity of the one person was interfering with a great act of inter-personal giving. If a person could give up his whole life for a friend, could he not also give up a kidney? The problem was solved, in my opinion, by a narrower definition of mutilation. Transplantation thus was seen as an act of charity; the principle of totality saw the good of more than one person at stake. Thus transplantation was no longer seen as a mutilation and the principle condemning mutilation still stood. In answer to the question, "What's going on here?" it could be answered, "Not just skin-slitting, not just removal of an organ but a life-saving transfer of organs which have no value of themselves but only insofar as they promote human life. We are now promoting two human lives at the expense of no true human value." Fine.

In analyzing what has happened here, we have to realize that certain words already define the human act; that is, they already have attached a value to the action. For example, murder, rape, arson, and mutilation. To describe an act as a mutilation is to say that there is something wrong with it, that it's bad as a totality. This is important, for if in answer to the question, "What's going on here?" the doctor answered, "I'm mutilating one person, but it's for a good purpose. We're saving somebody else's life," we would have a clear example of the classic "bad means" for a "good end." That's why it was necessary to be able to see the transplant operation not as (1) a mutilation and (2) then a life-saver but as one inter-personal act which really did no evil and accomplished much good. Again, so far no problem.

The problem comes in the extension of the principle of the "total human act."

"What's going on here?"
"I'm making the world a better place to live."
"Could you be a bit more specific?"
"Sure, I just sent 500 inmates of a mental institution to their heavenly reward. Yesterday I eliminated quite a bit of suffering, worry, and even some despair by speeding up the journey to heaven for 54 people in an old folks home . . . ."

"What's going on here?"
"I'm making the world peaceful."
"Could you be a bit more specific?"

"Sure, I just sent off some H-bombs to eliminate all the political centers of Russia, China, and Albania."

"Oh no! Your good purpose just can't justify your means!"

"Are you ever old fashioned! You're dividing up into unrealistic categories my total human act which is really one of peace-making."

These examples may seem too far-fetched. Let's take a look at what actually has happened.

"What's going on here?"

"We're just following orders."

"Could you be more specific?"

"Sure. We're eliminating a problem?"

"What sort of a problem?"

"The 'Jewish problem.' You're looking at 5000 Jews about to be eliminated." (Actual total: 6,000,000)

Or again, listen to the proponents of abortion, not 5 years from now, but in the legislative debates for social abortion.

"What's going on here?"

"I'm building family happiness."

"Could you be more specific?"

"Sure. I'm a doctor; I'm performing a perfectly legal abortion."

"That's building family happiness?"

"Sure. This woman figured that the family budget was already tight enough. She didn't take the pill one day, got pregnant and very unhappy. She began to take out her unhappiness on the rest of the family. Everybody got unhappy. So by aborting her, I'm building family happiness."

"Yes, but what about the right of the unborn baby?"

"Look. Today you've got to look at the big picture, the total human act. We're not takers of innocent human life. We're builders of happiness . . . ."

To bring in these examples is not to bring in a red herring. They illustrate the actual evil that has come from misapplication of this principle of the total human act. One can say that there is no intrinsic connection between contraception and abortion, but there is a bridge, and that bridge is the approach to the problem. An approach which glides over the evil of certain specific actions by saying that they take their morality from the larger, total human act is erroneous, misleading, and ultimately destructive of morality.

Nor is it an adequate answer to imply that the limiting criteria is human acceptability. "If doctors decide that the removal of a foetus is medically necessary, and if this is humanly acceptable, then it *is not* abortion (except perhaps in purely medical or physiological terms), and the principle that abortion is murder, still applies." [2] What is "humanly acceptable?" In a recent book, Msgr. Paul Furfey [3] admirably demonstrated the gross evils that have become "humanly acceptable" to people well-educated in the western (Judeo-Christian?) culture. I shall never forget an abortion symposium held at the University of Santa Clara in early 1967. A respectable doctor said he wanted abortion legalized to make legal what he and his colleagues were already doing. A respectable sociologist told us about his gardening — how you have to thin out the rows of carrots so the survivors will have more room to grow. He didn't verbalize his conclusion about humans; — he didn't have to. Finally, an Episcopalian priest (Rev. Charles Carroll) who had been at the Nuremberg trials arose to express his shock at such reasoning and to express his fears concerning the similarity between the solution of the problem of the undesired child in the womb and the solution of the problem of the undesired Jews (by the Nazis) in Germany.

It is absolutely necessary to focus attention on the lowest level of a meaningful human act in its materiality in order to keep the principle of the total human act from degenerating into a broad-brush morality of good intentions. What does this mean? Let's use some examples.

---

2. Van der Marck, *Love and Fertility* (London: Sheed & Ward, 1965), p. 60.
3. *The Respectable Murderers* (New York: Herder & Herder, 1965).

John Doe has just pushed a button. That button activated an electrical circuit which sent a missile with an H-bomb warhead to Peking. Ths description is completely material. It becomes interpretive or "intentional" when that button pushing is described as "making the world peaceful" or "eliminating a source of great tension."

The meaningful material act here is not "button pushing" but "H-bombing Peking." Thus it would be erroneous on the side of materiality to isolate "button pushing" as the "lowest level of a meaningful human act." It would be erroneous on the side of "totality" to describe it in the interpretative terms "making the world peaceful." The act must be evaluated on the morality of H-bombing Peking.

Dr. Smith has just performed a surgical procedure in which he directly extinguished the life of a three week old human being. The lowest level meaningful human act here is the killing of the young human being. An interpretive description would call this either "murder" or "aiding the health of the mother" or "building family happiness." It would be erroneous on the side of materiality to describe the act as "the removal of a foetus" and erroneous on the side of intentionality to describe the act as "building family happiness." The morality of the human act of killing a young human being will be judged on principles that can be applied to other cases where the direct killing of a human life is "justified" . . . self-defense and capital punishment.

What has all this to do with the controversy on contraception? In this area an effort is made to look at marriage as one totality, which in one respect is obviously quite true. It is then asserted that what is important is not the contraceptive character of individual acts but whether or not the marriage as a whole is open to life. In this view, the individual marital sex acts are important as regular expressions of affective love but unimportant from the point of view of procreation.

It would seem that we are dealing with a new form of double standard in sex morality. The individual act is seen as significant from the point of view of personal love but not significant from the point of view of procreation. In the latter case it would seem that this theory regards as significant only the totality of the marriage.

The error of this double standard can be illustrated by another violation of the marriage covenant. Is fidelity to be judged only by the totality of the marriage or by individual acts? If one spouse engages in occasional acts of adultery, is that spouse guilty of wrong-doing, or infidelity? Or should these individual acts be considered as an insignificant level of activity because the only significant level is the "total human act of the whole marriage" which was faithful most of the time? Granted the importance of the "most of the time" fidelity, does this make the individual act of adultery not significant, not objectively immoral?

Setting a double standard for the evaluation of individual sex acts is an erroneous solution to the problem. If it is argued that there is no double standard, that the individual sex act is not seen as important or significant from the point of view of personal love (just as it is not seen as significant from the point of view of procreation), two things need to be asked: (1) If it is not important, then why be concerned about not having it? (2) On what basis does one assume or prove that the individual sex act is not a significant total human act?

The assumption that the individual sex act does need to be regarded as a significant level of human action, a total interpersonal human act in its own right is the weakest point in this line of reasoning. From the most cursory survey of modern literature, theatre and movies, it would seem self-evident that sex activity, in its individual acts, has caused and continues to cause so much concern that it needs to be considered always as significant. I cannot see how its significance is lessened by its commonness, nor can I agree that its basic significance is reduced by such obvious distortions as rape and prostitution. The reason why these are abhorrent is that we understand that in the order of creation the sex act is *meant to be* a significant interpersonal activity and that these are gross contradictions of the intended meaning.

Another flaw in this argument is that it glosses over the violation of the totality of the individual marriage act while concentrating on the totality of the marriage. The totality of the individual act is that it is both open to interpersonal love and to the possibility of life.

The problem of contraception really boils down to how we should answer the question, "What's going on here?" about the sex act. It would be an error on the side of materiality to describe the act as the insertion of the penis in the vagina with subsequent ejaculation of semen therein. It is an error on the side of intentionality to describe the action as one of making love, for love is what is hoped for or intended. The same would be true of a description which called the action one of developing our personalities, expressing our affection, expressing our love.

An accurate description must include the relevant circumstances. Each of the above intentional descriptions could have been said by a couple not married to each other. At the minimum then, an accurate description must include whether or not the sex act takes place within marriage.

The key question in the contraceptive controversy is whether or not an accurate description of the married sex act also needs to include the circumstance of contraception, that is, whether the morality of the action is affected by that particular circumstance. Is contraception relevant or not in the evaluation of the moral character of the marital sex act?

In my opinion it is. I think that a valid description of the morally good marital sex act has to read something like this: an act of sexual, mutually genital, intercourse which is intended to express marital feelings of affection and which does not positively exclude the possibility of procreation. I have deliberately omitted the word love, for to insert it would be begging the question, "When is sexual activity truly human love activity?"

In summary, I do not think that those who advocate the extension of the principle of the total human act to contraception have proved by any means that it is a legitimate extension. Quite obviously, Pope Paul VI doesn't think so either, for he specifically criticizes the contraceptive misapplication in his encyclical, *Humanae Vitae.*

Finally, I do not think that the advocates of intersubjectivity and total human act have showed us that we can discard the "end and means approach." Certainly it is necessary to see an action in its totality; but it is equally necessary to limit that totality to the lowest meaningful level of material human activity.[4] It is likewise necessary, when thinking about human actions to distinguish between the materiality and the intention, the physical means and the human intention. Without such distractions we will have a fuzzy morality of good intentions in which the grand over-all purpose will be seen to specify all the lesser level acts. This "grand purpose morality" is clearly rejected by those who object to immoral acts in a war which may be "justified" on the

---

4. There is a fast growing tendency among the advocates of the principle of the total human act to consider some material sexual activity as not a human act. The favorite example is masturbation. "One moralist maintains that masturbation for seminal analysis is not morally wrong. Just a human consideration, now buttressed by modern psychology, indicates that such an act is not the human act of masturbation. Even though the act has the same material substratum as masturbation, the human act in this case is an act of obtaining semen for analysis." The quote is from Charles Curran, *Christian Morality Today* (Notre Dame, Ind.: Fides Publishers, Inc., 1966), p. 129. He identifies the theologian as Bernard Häring, C.Ss.R., who proposed such an opinion as probable at Regis College, Toronto, July, 1963. I cannot help thinking that this is word changing without reality changing. No longer is the act of self-stimulus for orgasm seen as a meaningful human act. It is judged only on the basis of the overall purpose — semen analysis, fertility study, etc. If this is the case then the act of self-stimulus for orgasm is not wrong in itself. Only when it is done for "selfish" reasons is it called by the negative value word of "masturbation." And if it is not selfish to obtain semen through voluntary orgasm instead of more bothersome methods, then how could it be termed selfish for a man to seek simple relief from sexual tension rather than the more bothersome way of sweating it out? We have now developed a whole new criteria of morality: "selfishness." However, selfishness is a purely intentional aspect, and a morality of "selfishness" errs by neglecting the material (means) and stressing only the intention (end). This leaves me with the opinion that all willful sex activity is at the level of a meaningful human act whose morality is judged by the marriage covenant, not by other circumstances such as seminal analysis and relief of tensions.

whole; it must also be rejected in other areas of interpersonal relations including sex.

6.   Conscience

In the entire contraception controversy, the place of conscience is respected by all. Everyone admits that the individual person must follow the dictates of his personal conscience. That has been axiomatic among Catholics even to the extent that the Catholic high school or college student will probably be told that if in conscience he no longer believes in the divinity of Christ, then he must follow his conscience, even though erroneous, and leave the Church. So conscience must be followed, even when it is wrongly informed. Thus it is misleading to ask a theologically informed person if he believes, in the last analysis, that the decision on contraception must be left to the individual conscience. Even a non-contraceptionist must answer "Yes" to that; but he or she may very well want to add, "And the same holds true for the decision whether to steal this particular car, or have relations with this particular unmarried woman now."

The question is more accurately stated, "How can I know if I have a properly informed conscience? Which voice among all the many voices clamoring for attention is the voice of God? Am I in my conscience acting like Adam who wanted to be like God, knowing for himself what was right and wrong, independently of God? Or am I being like Christ who said only 'Not my will but yours be done.' "

Two avenues must be explored. In the first place, there is a myriad of decisions of conscience where about the only hope for objectively good action lies in a person who understands the problem well *and* who has developed the habit or virtue of acting morally in this sort of situation. Secondly, there are those problems which are specific enough and have been considered long enough to be the subject of the universal negative teaching of the Church, whether it be explicitly contained in her Scriptures or has developed in her Tradition, e.g., "Thou shall not murder."

The question about contraception boils down to the truth and the force of the prohibition: "Thou shall not practice artificial contraception."

In the first instance, the contraception controversy is clearly a matter of Christian marital chastity. In order both to think truthfully and to act morally in this matter, one must possess the virtue of chastity. Father Van der Marck sums it up in the statement: "Human action does not proceed from knowledge but from habit or virtue." [5] If one's actions do not flow from the virtue of marital chastity, if one's ideas about marital love are biased because of the fog of egocentricism, then one will not arrive at the truth about married love. This is by no means to infer that everyone who arrives at an erroneous idea about married love is unchaste; rather it is to say that it would seem very difficult for persons involved in habits of marital unchastity to arrive at true speculative judgments about marital chastity when in the existential order their practical judgments would either have to change or be tinged with guilt.

In the second instance we are concerned with the truth and consequent force of the Church's authoritative prohibition of artificial birth control, contraception. In forming a correct conscience, how much weight should be given to this teaching? Should it be regarded as the fruit of the workings of the Holy Spirit, and therefore true, and thus absolutely normative and formative for one's conscience? Or should it be regarded as merely the fruit of the workings of some conservative theologians, at the best an example of limited human wisdom, and therefore not necessarily true, and thus not normative and formative for one's conscience? (To regard it as a "probable opinion" is to accept the second alternative.)

Much ink and many words have told all who can hear that the papal teaching is not an "infallible" teaching. That, as I said earlier (Chapter One), is not fully accurate. It is not a "defined" teaching, and therefore we do not have the highest certitude of

---

5. William H. Van der Marck, O.P., *Toward a Christian Ethic* (Paramus, N.J.: Paulist/Newman Press, 1967), p. 152.

faith that it is infallibly true. Thus we cannot be accurate in saying that the teaching is or isn't infallible, i.e., infallibly true. We can only say that we cannot say *with the certainty of faith* one way or the other. If it is true, it is infallibly true; but we may not know it with the certainty of faith, ever — or at least until it is *defined* as true.

The fact that the doctrine of non-contraception is not a "defined" dogma is *almost* irrelevant. What if it were "defined?" It would *still* be a matter of conscience, just as it is a matter of conscience to believe in the full divinity and full humanity of Christ. The difference, of course, is that when something has been defined we have the final certitude of faith that it is true. Where something is a subject of the *ordinary* magisterium there is the theoretical possibility that the doctrine may be changed under the same or different circumstances.

Still the Catholic knows that he can approach the work of the ordinary magisterium secure in the belief that the magisterium gives him the practical certainty he needs for acting. If he has intellectual differences with the reasoning of a particular teaching or with its conclusion, he must realize that the burden of proof is on him. One is simply not morally free, as a Catholic, to act contrary to the explicit teaching of a clarified magisterium (as opposed to a magisterium in doubt) unless there is overwhelming evidence that the ordinary magisterium has erred. He must rather give the presumption to the guidance of the Church by the Holy Spirit.

There is nothing new in any of this. Even the proponents of dissent acknowledge that the papal teaching office cannot be regarded just as the voice of another theologian and that there must always be sufficient reasons for dissent.[6] Given a religious faith which was born on the cross and constantly remains under the sign and shadow of the cross, the presence of great difficulty is not of itself sufficient reason for dissent from an authoritative teaching of the magisterium. Nor is there sufficient reason simply

---

6. Charles E. Curran, *Contraception: Authority and Dissent* (New York: Herder & Herder, 1969), pp. 9-10.

because of alleged defects in the reasoning used by the Pope in this case. It seems to me that "sufficient reason" must include both error in the reasons put forth by the papal teaching office *and* a case for the contrary doctrine which is overwhelmingly convincing. Whether the critics of *Humanae Vitae* have succeeded in showing that it's reasoning process was erroneous is debatable. That they have not yet succeeded in formulating an overwhelmingly convincing contrary doctrine is certain. Thus I cannot agree that there is ample evidence for believing that the papal office has erred in affirming the tradition of non-contraception even though I personally prefer another way of explaining such a doctrine. (If I felt that the present official explanation was entirely satisfactory for our day, I certainly wouldn't be writing this book.)

Lastly, it should be noted that it will be humanly impossible, considering our passions and the difficulty with which we come to the truth, to have a properly formed Christian conscience without the faith which comes from hearing (Rom 10:17). To possess a true conscience, one needs to listen to the truth which is illuminated by the action of the Holy Spirit who guides the teaching of the Catholic Church.

In summary, everyone must follow his conscience. He has an equal obligation to make sure that his conscience is properly informed. This he can do only through faith. A cornerstone of the Catholic faith is the belief that it is the community established by Christ and led by the Holy Spirit. We have the highest certitude of faith in a teaching that comes through an *ex cathedra* definition of Pope or Council. We have the practical certitude for action in those teachings which are not *ex cathedra* but are taught authoritatively by the magisterium. In these cases, the presumption is that the Holy Spirit is operative. The strength of the teaching is not its theological argumentation but rather the believed backing of the Holy Spirit.

The burden of proof lies on those who would seek to change a teaching of the magisterium. On the basis of the arguments advanced thus far in the controversy, one is forced to conclude that the contraceptionists have not succeeded at all well in showing that contraception is morally good or that the principles which they enunciate are validly applied to this question or that they will not cause moral havoc when applied in other areas.

7.   The Principle of the Overriding Right

Among the efforts to provide a way out of the apparent impasse between the doctrine of non-contraception and the difficulties of married couples in living it, some attempts have been made in the way of formulating general principles that would be applicable to moral behavior as a whole. These efforts keep the traditional moral doctrines intact but limit their applicability. It seems to me that this approach has a chance of bearing fruit. It does not treat contraception as a unique case and then develop principles for it alone, principles which can cause havoc when applied to other areas of human life. Instead it starts with the treatment of contraception as one problem among many.

One such effort has been made by Denis E. Hurley, O.M.I., Archbishop of Durban, in his formulation of the principle of over-riding right.[7] In his own words,

> The principle of the overriding right boils down to this. Situations arise in life when a right clashes with a duty. For instance, when I am attacked, my right to life clashes with my duty to respect the life of another; when I am in dire need, my right to life clashes with my duty to respect the property of another; when an infected organ threatens my life, my right to life clashes with my duty to preserve my bodily integrity; when I am bound by secrecy, my right to preserve the secret may clash with my duty to tell the truth. In all these cases we admit that the right predominates over the duty. This seems to indicate that we need to formulate the general principle underlying these various particular convictions. The formulation I proposed was "When the infringement of an obligation is necessarily involved in the exercise of a proportion-

---

7. *Furrow,* 17 (October, 1966), pp. 619-622.

ate right, the obligation ceases." I suggested that this principle might be useful in solving the moral problems of contraception, sterilization, and transplantation of organs from living people.[8]

The principle had been criticized by Richard A. McCormick, S.J. who did not see it as the answer to the present dilemma.[9] My own criticism is that I think Archbishop Hurley makes a false antithesis between rights and duties. In each of the examples he uses, it would have been just as proper to speak of the clash between *my duty* "to preserve my own life" and *my duty* "to respect the life of another"; . . . *my duty* "to preserve my life and my duty to preserve my bodily integrity"; . . . *my duty* "to preserve the secret" and *my duty* "to tell the truth." I don't think this is just a matter of splitting hairs but of trying to put the contrasting elements of a human situation in terms of a common denominator so that evaluation can proceed more rationally and without the emotional connotations involved in the statement of a dilemma in terms of rights versus duties.

Archbishop Hurley criticizes the application of the principle of totality to the corporate person of the family. He wonders if there is "anything to prevent its being applied to the corporate person of the state? Unless it is very carefully formulated, it may very well become a principle of totalitarianism. We should beware, therefore, of invoking the principle of totality in respect of collectivities until we have discovered a foolproof formulation — which I suspect will be very hard to find." [10]

The same criticism is to be made of his own formulation, and he admits as much. Just as the principle of totality is accepted in theory by all but disputed in its application, so also with the principle of the overriding right (or duty). What I find helpful about Archbishop Hurley's effort is that it doesn't want simply

---

8. "In Defense of the Principle of Overriding Right," *Theological Studies,* 29 (June, 1968), p. 301.

9. *Theological Studies,* 28 (December, 1967), pp. 757-758.

10. *Theological Studies,* 29 (June, 1968), p. 305.

to change the teaching or to treat contraception as an isolated ethical problem. Rather he attempts to formulate a broad principle, which may or may not ever be applicable to the contraception question, but which at least may be a step in the right direction in the over-all efforts of moral theology.

8.   The Principle of Compromise

Other efforts to arrive at a way out of the dilemma of many couples include formulations of a principle of compromise (Charles Curran) [11] and a principle of tension (Peter Chirico, S.S.).[12] Both of these efforts share the value that they are not isolated treatments of the contraceptive problem but rather the formulation of wider principles that can be applied to a whole range of moral crises. On the other hand, both share the common difficulty of being an interpretation of how people *have made* their decisions rather than being a guide as to how one *should* make decisions. That is, neither attempt offers much practical guidance in forming one's conscience. Neither helps in the determination of the higher or lower values. They are principles insofar as they provide a guide for the analysis of moral guilt but not insofar as they provide a guide for determining the right and obligatory thing to do.[13]

Both share another common advantage and fault. They both lay emphasis on man's sinful condition in an imperfect world. They recognize that contraception is an evil, and they justify it on the basis of man's state of imperfection and other evils in his situation. On the other hand, such an emphasis can tend towards a mystique of sin, a feeling that there is really no point in developing the virtues because the more we sin, the more we

11. Charles E. Curran, "Dialogue with Joseph Fletcher," *Homiletic and Pastoral Review*, 67 (1967), pp. 821-829.
12. Peter Chirico, S.S., "Tension, Morality, and Birth Control," *Theological Studies*, 28 (1967), pp. 258-285.
13. Richard A. McCormick, S.J., *Theological Studies, 28* (December, 1967), pp. 759-760.

have to admit our need of God and the more we feel his gracious, forgiving presence.

Such arguments are taking place in the theological community at the present time, and I personally regard them as more helpful and more hopeful than the arguments that I have seen dealing rather exclusively with contraception. They may also be more dangerous, but at least they may be evaluated in an atmosphere that is less charged with emotion than that surrounding the contraception controversy.

9. The Papal Birth Control Commission Report

The core of the controversy as reflected in the contrasting reports by members of the Papal Birth Control Commission centers around one paragraph in the "position paper" signed by Revs. Joseph Fuchs, S.J., Canon Phillippe Delhaye, and Raymond Sigmond, O.P. It is inserted as a *Explanatory Note* in "Section III. *Intervention is well explained within the limits of the classic doctrine.*"

Not every act which proceeds from man is a complete human act. The subject of morality for St. Thomas is always the human act whose master is man (determined from a knowledge of the object or end). But this human act which has one moral specification can be composed of several particular acts *if these partial acts do not have some object in itself already morally specified.* And this is the case for matrimonial acts which are composed of several fertile and infertile acts; they constitute one totality because they are referred to one deliberate choice. (Emphasis added) [14]

I don't think it any sort of an oversimplification to say that the controversy is summed up in the last sentence. Is it true that

---

14. Robert G. Hoyt (ed.), *The Birth Control Debate* (Kansas City, Mo.: National Catholic Reporter, 1968), p. 72.

all the matrimonial acts — fertile, naturally infertile, and deliberately infertile (contraceptive) are all just one totality? I have already shown why the advocates of contraception do not have a valid application of the principle of totality. In terms of their own philosophy, I would answer that the individual sex act is not a partial act but in itself is already morally specified. I believe that this specification is conferred first of all by the marriage covenant which makes of the sex act a sacramental encounter. As such, each and every exercise of the sex act in marriage has its own particular value and structure; each and every sex act is meaningful in itself, or at least meant to be meaningful in itself.

Aside from the inadequacy of the argument from totality in this regard, the majority reports carry other interesting features. Regarding abstinence, married people are said to recognize that they must abstain sometimes for lengthy periods of time because of various conditions of their lives including "professional necessities." However according to the sense of the faithful, "condemnation of a couple to a long and often heroic abstinence as the means to regulate conception cannot be founded on the truth." Abstinence for professional reasons is acceptable; abstinence for religious reasons is questioned, while the debatable sense of the faithful seems to be accepted as determinative.

Another interesting feature is the analysis of the objective criteria of morality. *Gaudium et Spes* (Par. 51) mentions the necessity of objective criteria: "Therefore when there is question of harmonizing conjugal love with the responsible transmission of life, the moral aspect of any procedure does not depend solely on sincere intentions or on an evaluation of motives. It must be determined by objective standards. These, based on the nature of the human person and his acts, preserve the full sense of mutual self-giving and human procreation in the context of true love. Such a goal cannot be achieved unless the virtue of conjugal chastity is sincerely practiced."

The majority papers twice list their interpretation of objective criteria. In the first instance they are given as follows:

3. *Objective criteria for the moral decision concerning methods.*

(1) Infecundity of the act, when this is required by right reason, should be accomplished by an intervention with lesser inconveniences to the subject. Man can use his body in such a way as to render it more apt to attain its proper ends but he cannot manipulate his body and organs in an arbitrary fashion.

(2) If nature ought to be perfected, then it should be perfected in the manner more fitting and connatural.

(3) On the other hand, this intervention ought to be done in a way more conformed to the expression of love and to respect for the dignity of the partner.

(4) Finally, efficacity should also be considered. If there is privation of conception for the sake of procuring other goods, these must be sought in a more secure and apt manner.

In this matter the rhythm method is very deficient. Besides only 60 per cent of women have a regular cycle.[15]

The second instance occurs in the final report.

(1) "The action must correspond to the nature of the person and of his acts so that the whole meaning of the mutual giving and of human procreation is kept in a context of true love.

(2) "The means which are chosen should have an effectiveness proportionate to the degree of right or necessity of averting a new conception temporarily or permanently.

(3) "The means to be chosen, where several are possible, is that which carries with it the least possible negative element, according to the concrete situation of the couple.

(4) "Then, in choosing concretely among means, much depends on what means may be available in a certain region or at a certain time or for a certain couple; and this may depend on the economic situation." [16]

---

15. *Ibid.*, p. 75 .
16. *Ibid.*, p. 94 .

In the first list, we are told (1) to choose the method most convenient, (2) to choose the method most fitting and connatural (3) to be dignified and loving and (4) to be efficient.

In the second list, #1 is almost a verbatim quote from *Gaudium et Spes*. As such it offers no interpretation; #2 says to be as efficient as you have to be; #3 says to choose the means that are the least obnoxious; #4 says to choose what you can afford from what's available.

First of all, how can these be considered any realistic sort of objective criteria? In the first list, numbers 2, 3, and 4 are really as much subjective as objective. The individual couple decide how efficient they want to be, what seems least negative and what they can afford. In the second list, "lesser inconveniences" is surely a subjective element. What is "fitting and connatural" and "conformed to the expression of love . . ." is begging the question. As such it offers no objective criteria. Lastly efficiency is both subjective and objective, but it has nothing to do with chastity. Argumentation which confuses objective with subjective and comes out with a totality that is in perfect agreement with hard-core pragmatism and then calls this the criteria for chastity surely does not recommend itself very well to a Christian people searching for truth and virtue.

The minority position paper signed by Revs. John Ford, S.J., Jan Visser, C.Ss.R., Marcelino Zalba, S.J., and Stanislaus de Lestapis, S.J., has been amply criticized. The primary criticism has been that their report skipped over the problem of contraception and focused only on the fact of the tradition and the teaching authority of the Church. The criticism is not wholly accurate. Their report is divided into two sections. Part I is concerned with the tradition and authority. Part II, almost as long as Part I, is concerned with the argumentation of the advocates of contraception. It includes references to the magisterium but is primarily concerned with philosophical and moral questions. One may disagree with the authors' treatment, but it is not fair to say that they have not handled the problem.

Furthermore, the minority paper of Ford and others raises

some questions to which the position paper of Fuchs and others failed to give an adequate response. For example, the Ford paper alleges that the reasoning process of the contraception theorists logically opened the door to permitting non-marital relations, oral and anal intercourse, masturbation and direct sterilization. The Fuchs paper apparently accepts the charge about direct sterilization as falling under the objective criteria of efficiency. The other answers are worth looking at in quotation.[17]

> b. The so-called new theory is extremely strict, as is that of the casuists, with regards to oral and anal copulation, *since it does not permit them*. For in these acts there is preserved neither the dignity of love nor the dignity of the spouse as human persons created according to the image of God. (Emphasis added)

The answer is inadequate because it is arbitrary, authoritarian, and reneges on their basic argument from totality. On what criteria is it established that in these acts the dignity of love and of the spouses is not preserved? If a couple thinks it helps their interpersonal relationship, who can fault them? Or again, under the principle of totality, such acts would have to be seen as taking their virtue from the overall totality of all the sex acts. Of themselves, they would only be a partial act, not a true human act, so there would be no reason not to permit them.

> c. Human intervention in the process of conception is not permitted, as we have said, unless it favors the stability of the family. Therefore there is no parity with the question of extra-marital relations. These relations lack the sense of complete and irrevocable giving and the possibility of normally accepting and educating children. These extra-marital relations contradict the norms already given concerning the habitual ordination of the institution of marriage towards offspring and love.

---

17. *Ibid.*, pp. 76-77.

Yes, but why? If, under the principle of totality, individual sex acts are only partial human acts and get their specific morality from the totality of marriage acts, why become concerned about a "little" bit of adultery. The contraception theory has already admitted the acceptability of individual contraceptive acts which by definition "lack the sense of complete and irrevocable giving and the possibility of normally accepting and educating children." It sees these as imperfect acts made perfect by the overall fecundity and self-giving of the total marriage. If the authors of the theory had spoken with the prostitutes interviewed by one of the San Francisco papers some time ago, they would have become aware that a fair share of the clientele are happily married men whose wives are pregnant and who felt that for family stability it would be good to have relief from sexual tensions. Furthermore, it is very questionable whether a marriage which is positively contraceptive in some ninety percent of its sexual acts can really be described as having an "habitual ordination . . . towards off-spring." Whether we like it or not, that is the real alternative to the traditional doctrine, one which is being lived and preached by countless thousands.

d. The affirmation of the permissibility of intervention does not lead to an indulgent attitude towards masturbation since intervention preserves the intersubjectivity of sexuality (they shall be two in one flesh). Masturbation rather negates that intersubjectivity. Masturbation in as much as it turns the individual on himself and seeks mere egocentric satisfaction, totally perverts the essential intentionality of sexuality whereby man is directed out of himself towards another. For intercourse even with intervention is self-giving and heterosexual. If a question is to be raised about masturbation, this should be done independently of the question of the regulation of birth, even should the classic teaching on this matter remain in force.

The answer fails to meet the objection. First of all, the objection by Ford *et al* didn't raise the question of masturbation for egocentric satisfaction but rather as motivated by the same reasons given for the licitness of contraception. The objection envisioned a situation wherein physical illness might preclude any marital relations and where the sexual tensions that play such a big part in the contraceptive theory would build up. Masturbation would then be used to release sexual tension in order to have better family stability. If the marriage was normally heterosexual, the theory that individual acts are only partial acts receiving their morality from the totality would certainly seem to allow the partial act of masturbation.

The statement that "intercourse even with intervention is self-giving and heterosexual" is most unfortunate. Obviously the married contraceptive act is heterosexual, but it is erroneous to say that it is self-offering. Contraceptive *or open to life,* it is simply näive to assume that intercourse, even between married people, is self-offering. It is *meant to be* that, but the whole question of the morality of any given sex act in marriage is whether or not it is *actually* an act of self-offering. The contraceptive question itself can be stated in terms of self-offering: Is an act which by positive intervention excludes any possibility of new life a real self-offering or is it rather a form of mutual enjoyment or even use? Does the reality (contraception) make a mockery of the sign (self-giving)?

With the case for contraception based on an unacceptable extension of the principle of totality and upon näive and erroneous statements about the sex act itself, it should hardly be surprising that Pope Paul felt constrained to reject the contraceptive conclusion. To overturn the tradition on the basis of arguments that could be faulted as easily as those presented him by members of the Commission would be theologically irresponsible.

On the other hand, one can object that the natural law reasoning advanced by *Humanae Vitae* has failed to convince many of its own value. To an objective onlooker who did not feel qualified to pass judgment on the values of the arguments of either side, it would seem that the reasoning advanced by each position met with criticism and rejection by the other. It would seem that the dispute would never be settled on the grounds of reasoning alone. With an apparent holdoff at the philosophical level, (at least in the sense that each side's reasoning was unacceptable to the other) the issue needed clarification at some other level, the level of authority. Only an authoritative statement could break the apparent deadlock, and only through faith could this authoritative statement be accepted.

The function of *Humanae Vitae* was to reaffirm the doctrine of non-contraception. It did not ask for that highest type of faith, the faith given a dogmatic definition. Rather it asked for faith that the response of non-contraception given to a number of different questions over a period of some 1900 years was guided by the Holy Spirit. The issuance of *Humanae Vitae* said that the presumption of divine guidance had to be given to the tradition both because of the importance of that tradition, theologically speaking, and because the advocates of contraception had failed to produce logically convincing reasons for change. Instead, their reasons introduced principles capable of creating general moral havoc. The agony of the promulgation of *Humanae Vitae* was that the advocates of contraception had produced argument after argument to win the emotions and sympathies of all men. No one can deny the dimensions of the question, the worldwide problems connected with population density and the problems that go on in the homes of many married couples. Everyone would like to alleviate these things, especially if they could be alleviated by such a simple device as mechanical or chemical contraception. But instead of a teaching that would have been hailed as modern, scientific, and simple, we are left with a teaching that has no more sex appeal than the cross — folly to some and a stumbling block to others.

Chapter Five

TOWARD A UNIFIED THEORY OF CHRISTIAN
SEXUALITY

1. The Value and Limitation of a Theory

In the entire contraception controversy, there has been such
emphasis on the contraception problem of married people that
this problem has been isolated from the over-all problem of sex.
(Is there any age group over infancy and before senility for
which sex does not provide some sort of a challenge or problem?)
One serious aspect of this narrowing of perspective is that it
impedes the development of a theory of sex that can be applied to
the widest possible scope of sexual problems. Another serious
aspect of this restricted vision is that instead of seeing contraception in the light of an over-all theory of sex, theories are
developed to solve only the problem of contraception and are
then applied to other problem areas. For example, if one theorizes
that repression of the tendency to express affective love in intercourse is evil, the theory is very quickly applied to pre-marital
relations as well. Thus, while seeming to "solve" one problem,
the theory creates more.

One of the weaknesses inherent in much of the theorizing
that has taken place about contraception is that it has proceeded from the less known to the more known. That is, it has been
centered around contraception (a less known) and then is applied
to the more known (fornication, adultery), having the effect of

changing the traditional teaching on these as well (or at least not being able to show why they are evil).

A theory has value insofar as it applies to the greatest number of cases. The whole purpose of a theory, whether it be in the field of physics or morality, is to show a unifying theme, principle, or "law" which is applicable to all of the observable cases. In the physical sciences, the theory is first of all derived from observation. Then if more and new data are observed which do not fit into the previous formulation of the theory, an effort will be made to modify the theory or to replace it with a new one. However the new theory still has to explain the older data; it cannot rest content with an explanation which is suited only to the new observation. From the point of view of the "laws of the universe," a theoretical law attempts to account for the regular occurrences observed. If the statement of a "law" is changed, it is not because there was a change in nature but because new observations enabled the scientist to see more of nature and then forced him to account for the new observations as well as the old. A physical "law" is nothing more than a theoretical expression which has gained universal acceptance. It is an effort to explain that which *is* in the physical order, and the discovery of *physical being* in greater detail may well force the revision of previous theoretical statements which did not account for all that was there (but only that part which was initially observed).

A theory is more valuable if it is simple. The simpler it is, the more universal it will be, and the more universal, the more of *being* it will explain. The natural scientist yearns for the ultimate physical theory which will explain and unify everything. This of course will never eliminate the more complex and detailed explanations which are subordinate to, dependent upon, and congruent with the more general theory.

In the area of human behavior, the same is true. However, here we are aided immensely by God's self-revelation. We might say that instead of man searching endlessly for a final unifying theory to explain all human activity, God has given it free to man through his revelation that he is Love and that man is made in his image and likeness. However, this, if it be accepted as the prime theory, still leaves us with the duty of showing how various forms of behavior either are loving or are not loving, either do or do not enable man to live up to his calling to perfection in the likeness of Christ. Nor does the prime statement about man being made in the image and likeness of God who is Love spare us from the duty of trying to construct lesser and theoretical statements to cover both specific actions and whole areas of related activity.

2.   An Analysis of the Word "Love"

If one thing has become evident in the controversy on contraception and in the entire debate on ethics, it is that the word "love" has become meaningless for all practical purposes. Cardinal Suenens in his book *Love and Control* [1] recalled the story of the wise man who was asked what he would do if he had all the power in the world. The wise man answered that he would restore words to their original meanings. People commit crimes of "love"; they commit murder, theft and adultery for "love." Love in a certain sense has degenerated to meaning something someone likes to do because it might make him feel good in doing it.

In the area of sex, the sex act is frequently referred to as the act of "making love." It somehow implies that love can be produced by an action and that the repeated action produces a lover. Fortunately, the ordinary language of people gives a way of showing the falsity of this assumption.

(a) *Rape.* At the bottom of the moral scale of sex acts is forcible rape. This action involves the same anatomical act as that of two married persons, and it is possible that some acts of rape are conducted with less excitement and violence than some voluntary sex acts between married couples. But can people actually think that rape is expressive of love? You may want to answer

---

1. Leon J. Cardinal Suenens, *Love and Control* (Paramus, N.J.: Paulist/ Newman Press, 1961).

"NO!", but I remember a magazine article describing certain underprivileged people which leads me to think otherwise. In the case in mind, a young man raped a girl one night and then called her up the next night to ask for a date. It is not impossible that having been brainwashed about sex being "making love" that he might have thought that rape might be a "lovely" way of introducing himself. Then I have read that in the Sicilian culture it is not uncommon for a young man to rape a girl in order to get her hand in marriage. Apparently the stigma of rape is so bad for the girl that she has to become the rapist's wife or she will remain single for life. Yet, the very word "rape" in our ordinary language tells us that this is not what we mean by an act of love.

(b) *Fornication.* A considerable step up the scale is the voluntary sexual intercourse of two unmarried people. Even here we have to distinguish between the interpersonal relationship which is casual and that which is between two people who have signified their intention to become man and wife. And again, even in the casual relationship we have to distinguish between the one wherein the two people really like each other and the one in which one is effectively paying for the use of the other. I say that these forms are a step up the scale because at least they are generally mutually voluntary.

Our ordinary use of language puts prostitution at the bottom of this group. Is prostitution an act of love? Is it made so by having one party to the act say, "I made love so many times today?" or, "It cost me ten dollars to make love last night?" I think that the accumulated wisdom of ages has been reflected in our use of the word "prostitution" for this, a word which tells us of a complete disassociation of love and sexuality. In this particular case, and in others also, it is a shame that our genteel ears have refused to let our tongues use an expression which ordinary language has developed for many instances of sexual intercourse. The simple, straight-forward, Anglo-Saxon four letter word for fornication may be considered vulgar but it does a wonderful job of communicating. It says that the act wasn't really rape, but it certainly wasn't love either.

While condemning the act of prostitution as being a violation of the order of creation, we must be wary of condemning the prostitute. What if she is a victim of white slavery, afraid for her very life to run away? What if she has concluded that this is the only possible way in which she can support her children now that her husband has been killed? Fear, fear and more fear certainly will be taken into account by our heavenly Father in his judgment of those who violate one aspect of the interpersonal order of creation because they feel driven by other violations of that same order of creation.

There can be no denying the very real affection, liking, and desire that many unmarried people feel for each other and which they try to express in sexual intercourse. Is this really to be honored by the name of "love?" Again, our ordinary language has given us the word "fornication" to describe this sort of activity. "Fornication" is undoubtedly a value word; it says something besides "sexual intercourse," and it distinguishes this sort of affective behavior from that which takes place between two people married to each other.

Should "fornication" be used to describe sexual relations between people who have openly pledged to marry each other at a definite date in the future? (In my discussion, I will limit "pre-marital" to those circumstances). I have noticed at least one author who surmises that maybe St. Paul's condemnation of fornication *really* meant prostitution, and that therefore pre-marital relations are not forbidden by Sacred Scripture. But if fornication means prostitution, why do we have an ordinary language use of the two words, an ordinary person's understanding that these two words describe the sexual act in quite different circumstances? Certainly the word prostitution was available to St. Paul. Another possible explanation of why he specifically condemned fornication in Romans I and Galatians 5 while not specifically mentioning prostitution is that prostitution was probably admitted by all to be evil while there was a certain amount of pride and rationalization in fornication and in some of the other sins that he condemned.

In my opinion, pre-marital relations deserve to be described as fornication and fall under Paul's emphatic condemnation. However, even for those who want a special category for pre-marital relations (in the restricted sense of the term), it can be pointed out that the necessity for using "pre-marital" indicates that our ordinary language distinguishes between these pre-marital sex acts and those of the same couple after they are married. There is an ordinary common sense understanding that there is something morally defective about pre-marital relations, and this is backed up by the evident concern about pre-marital relations as indicated by the number of surveys which seek to identify such behavior.

I think that it is worthwhile to spend a moment on this. Here is a couple, John and Mary. They intend to be married in September. But now it is May. They love each other. They yearn for each other. They feel the psychological need for a concrete sign of being fully accepted by the other, a felt need which may completely pass once they are married. Why should they be deprived of this moment of sexual joy just because they haven't stood before the proper witnesses and exchanged their vows?

The answer is simple: they aren't married yet. They haven't yet "covenanted" with each other for life. All that they have done is to indicate in a non-binding way that they hope and intend to enter the marriage covenant in September. They are in no way ready to express a covenantal renewal until they have first of all entered something which they can then renew.

If they are ready to covenant and want to express their love in the sexual union, then they should immediately advance the date. It is a cruel misuse of terms to say that this couple is already "married," for if there is one thing which is common knowledge among ordinary folk, it is that you are free to back out anytime before you say "I do." It is the common understanding of mankind that the obligations of marital fidelity do not begin until the couple have formally married each other. By the same token, the right or privilege of expressing love in the sexual union does not begin until this couple has entered into the marriage covenant.

(c) *Adultery*. The old sin of adultery has been getting a new look lately. It is being seen not just as being unfaithful but is being looked upon as something positive, a love-refreshing relation which makes persons better able to cope with the problems of their individual marriages and careers. Episcopalian Bishop Pike [2] draws the example of a striving politician who is receiving one setback after another at a convention. A woman at the convention begins to work for him, offers to help in any way and then offers herself. (She has become unhappy with circumstances in her own marriage.) They bed down together. He rises psychologically recharged to fight the battle for good politics; she leaves with a new determination to make her own marriage go on. Neither other partner will ever know or will ever be "hurt"; it seems that nothing but good has come of it. Therefore, shouldn't we realize that "Thou shalt not commit adultery" should be modified with "most of the time" or "except under extenuating circumstances?"

At first glance it may seem that if nobody gets hurt, then so what? Hasn't the general purpose of the commandment been observed? Then we look a bit further. Why did Jesus tell us that even the adulterous intention was already the sin of adultery? Who was hurt by it? Only the one person involved who was injuring himself by his personal unchastity. The adulterous intention is not wrong simply because Jesus told us it was; he told us because it was wrong independently of his words. An ethic of "so long as nobody else gets hurt" cannot be reconciled with Scripture.

Because the two people in the adulterous union mentioned above supposedly gave each other a psychological boost and therefore "helped" each other, should we not admit that this was loving, helpful behavior? Should we not say then that this was not "adultery," a negative value description, but an act of authentic human love? Should we not admit that here we have a wonderful example of modern emancipation from a rigid ar-

---

2. James A. Pike, *You and the New Morality: 74 Cases* (New York: Harper & Row, 1967).

chaic code in favor of modern man who is self-determining and who must create his own life and values as he evolves and progresses? Certainly the adjectival approach (the use of such sympathy evoking words and phrases such as emancipation, archaic code, modern, self-determining, evolution, and progress) paves the way for a new interpretation of the commandment. However, the Christian must look at problems and solutions from within the context of salvation history. Here he finds that the important thing is the covenant relationship between God and his people. He finds in Hosea that the people's practice of idolatry is not called simply "idolatry" but is called adultery — because they have strayed from their covenant relationship; they have entered into other relationships which they considered more immediate and more helpful.

The case for adultery can be argued on all the personalist bases that are put forward for contraception. An outside affair might help avoid the greater evil of the marriage breaking up. An outside affair might aid in the personality development of the one; the two people who are not married to each other may genuinely love each other, may be willing to do anything for each other; why should they be restrained by a code kept alive in the Catholic Church by celibates? Why should they be stunted?

My answer is twofold. Our ordinary use of language sharply differentiates sexual relations between lovers who are married to each other and between lovers who are married to someone else. I believe a good case can be made for the fact that although prostitution is adultery when at least one party is married, the word "adultery" is ordinarily used to describe "non-professional" sexual relations. I believe that it carries in ordinary language the connotation of personal affection and desire. I think that adultery is more than just a seeking of relief; relief from sexual tension can be obtained through masturbation; I feel quite sure that generally adultery is more than just a physical relationship, that it usually is a personal relationship as well. Therefore I think that the common ordinary use of language has already taken into account the personalist reasons that can be argued and has called these interpersonal sexual relations "adultery."

The second part of my answer is that the interpersonal adulterous union violates the marriage covenant which calls for fidelity in season and out of season, in tension and without tension, in periods of affection and in those unfortunate periods of mutual or unilateral irritation or plain boredom.

In all of the instances we have looked at, we have seen sexuality in action. In each instance, we have tried to show that there is a disassociation between sexuality and authentic human love. Because all of them go at times under the label of "making love," we have tried to show that in our ordinary language, mankind has always distinguished between sexuality and love by assigning the negative-value, non-love words of rape, prostitution, fornication, pre-marital sex, and adultery to these forms of sexual behavior. It should be self-evident by this time that there is no intrinsic link in practice between sexual behavior and love.

3.   A Covenant Theology of Love and Sexuality [3]

There are two questions which seem quite appropriate at this time. (1) In the interpersonal order of creation, is there meant to be an intrinsic link between sexuality and love? There can be sexual behavior without love and there can be love without sexual behavior, but my conviction is that sexual behavior is meant to be a manifestation of authentic human love. Through faith and conviction, I also hold that only within an authentic, valid marriage can sexual behavior be such an expression of love. (2) Within marriage, are sexual relations necessarily expressive of

---

3. When a theory of human behavior seeks to determine what is authentically loving behavior in terms of man's being made in the image and likeness of God and in terms of the Christian awareness that he is called to follow Christ, such a theory becomes a theology. Theology might very well be called a collection of theories attempting to throw light on man's relationships with God and creation, attempting to provide explanations of matters of faith and doctrine in the terms of the day. In the remainder of this chapter, the terms theory and theology are used interchangeably.

authentic married love? That is, just as outside of marriage, are there circumstances that need to be fulfilled for the meant-to-be order of creation to be present?

In the past pages I have frequently mentioned the marriage covenant, and many a reader will have already surmised the key to this theory of sex. It is simple. In the exchange of the marriage promises, the couple enter into a covenant with each other. The words they have uttered are a sacrament for though they are physical words they create a spiritual bond, a new relationship between this man and this woman. As sacramental, the promises signify what God is accomplishing in uniting this couple.

The covenant relationship is not just of their own making. It has a God-given structure; it is a relationship co-created both by God and by the man and wife. The man and woman must freely enter this relationship; they must make the God-intended relationship their own or there is no real covenant but just a meaningless and hypocritical ceremony. By the same token, they do not make their own unique covenant without reference to the structure intended by God. If, for example, they agreed in all sincerity that if they were to lose mutual love and affection for each other sometime in the future they would feel free to find other mates, there simply would be no covenant of marriage. It might be a commonly accepted social custom, it might be more accurately called a state of respectable mistressing or fornication; it simply is not a marriage. God does not marry two people unless they want it; the two people cannot marry unless they are willing to enter into the relationship that God has intended.

(a) *The Marriage Covenant.* What does this covenant entail? The contraception controversy thus far has highlighted two aspects of the marriage covenant: the willingness to help each other to grow in love and the willingness to let love produce life — which in turn calls for more love from the married couple. I would like to draw attention to the specific conditions under which the couple marry. They promise each other that they marry each other with all that is entailed in the marriage covenant *without reservation;* specifically — for richer and for poorer, in sickness and in health, for better and for worse as long as they are both still living. Needless to say, both persons are probably hoping that everything works out for better, healthier and richer. Nevertheless, it is their willingness to give of each other without serious reservation that makes the marriage. It is their willingness to accept each other, to remain faithful to each other, and to be still loving to the other under difficult and even disastrous circumstances, and to do this until they are separated by death that makes their union a marriage. It is these qualities that make their union an authentic permanent love-union and not just a socially and economically acceptable liaison or long term affair.

Because they have now entered into a marriage relationship, a mutual personal commitment of lifelong love without reservation, they are now free to express that union sacramentally in the sexual union. The sex-union now becomes a physical way of expressing their marriage covenant. The sex-union now says, "We are together; we are committed to each other; we are to love each other and we hope we *do* love each other without reservation, for better and for worse, whatever that may entail. Amen." The sex-union now is morally good because it is the renewal of the marriage covenant; it has become something more than physical; it has become sacramental, an outward expression of the interpersonal and God-made covenant of marriage. The criteria for evaluating sexual activity is not just physical; it is not just spiritual or intentional; it is sacramental which means that the criteria is truly human. It entails that wonderful inseparable union of sign and reality, matter and spirit, interpersonal relations with each other and with the Creator, human self-determination and fulfillment of the order created by God. The criterion that I propose for evaluating sexual activity is the marriage covenant itself. Sexual activity which renews the marriage covenant is morally good; sexual activity which does not renew the marriage covenant is morally evil.

(b) *Contraception and the Covenant.* How does contraception measure up against this criteria? First of all, I think it should be noted that when we are dealing with human actions we are not going to arrive at mathematical certainty. All we can do is show by analogy that a given mode of human behavior is contrary to the order of creation, and this holds true for the more gross and obvious forms of immorality such as murder as well as for the less obvious forms such as personal sins in the sexual order.

The argument against contraception here is by means of an analogy between the marriage covenant in the first place and the marital embrace as a renewal of that covenant. Any analysis of the reasons put forth for the practice of contraception finds them summarized as fear of consequences of ill health, fear of economic disadvantages, or fear of a number of things which can be called worse rather than better. Contraception is both a sign of refusal to run the risk of such consequences of the marital act and the means of absolutely and positively separating the unitive and procreative aspects of that marital act. By the use and the sign of contraception, the married couple using positive contraception have not renewed the marriage covenant in their marital relations. They have positively excluded in such relations all of the negative elements of the marriage covenant, those elements which call for a genuine self-giving love, those elements which require that they put their faith and their life-together in the hands of God. Their union is not a renewal of that great act of faith and risk they made when they covenanted with each other and with God. The contraceptive embrace positively excludes the necessity for that faith and confidence in the face of risk, that willingness to accept the difficult along with the sweet, that willingness which helped to make their union a marriage in the first place.[4]

By renewing only the "for better, for richer, and in health"

---

4. This is not to be understood as opposed to non-contraceptive responsible parenthood. I am not advocating a race to have the most babies to see who has the most trust in God. However, responsible parenthood first of all stems from responsible marriage. If comments which point up the risk involved in marriage serve to make some people think twice about marrying, I make no apologies. With the divorce rate in various states running from about one-half to almost equal the number of marriages, it is certainly time that more people gave the risks and

aspect of their covenant, and by positively excluding the "for worse, for poorer, and in sickness" aspect of that same covenant, it seems to me that the practitioners of contraception have invalidated this act which was meant to be a covenant-renewal "for richer *and* for poorer, in sickness *and* in health, for better *and* for worse" until by death do they part.

The immediate objection is that the practitioners of rhythm are doing the same thing. Here I think we have a clear advantage of using the marriage covenant as the criterion rather than using a comparison of various biological-chemical-physical methods of trying to avoid pregnancy. Using the marriage covenant, we can compare rhythm and contraception to the preparation for marriage. *(See Appendix I for updated treatment of "rhythm".)*

(c) *Pre-Marital Considerations.* In preparing for marriage, the love of most men and women is tempered or guided by some practicality and even fear. The typical man and woman will avoid selecting a mate who is ill. This may be completely unconscious, for the healthy person's dating pattern may automatically preclude getting to know an unhealthy person very well. The real test would come only if one party to a future marriage were suddenly stricken with a debilitating life-long disease. For example, what if the prospective groom suffered an accident and head injuries that would make it impossible for him ever to earn a living? Or what if the prospective bride were struck with a crippling disease that would not only make it impossible for her to care for children but even precluded the possibility of sexual relations? Would the remaining healthy prospective bride or groom be unloving not to enter marriage with the one who had met such a disaster? I, for one, couldn't judge non-marriage to be a sign of non-love in this case. I feel that in such heart-rending cases greater love may be shown by tender care and solicitude given

---

responsibilities of marriage more serious consideration. With contraception providing such an easy means of avoiding some of the chief responsibilities of marriage, I wonder if it has not also provided the means for the avoidance of such serious thought about marriage until it is too late.

without the bond of marriage than by entering a whole way of life under such circumstances. At any rate, before marriage, neither party has pledged life-long fidelity to the other, and both the one stricken and the one left healthy are free to break off the wedding plans.

Likewise, most people entering marriage give some attention to the economics of life together. "Will I be able to support a family without finishing my education? . . . Will I ever be able to support her with her background of having had everything she ever wanted and never having had to work for a cent? . . . Will he ever be able to support me and our children or will I have to be working all our married life? . . . Tom is studying to be a doctor; Jim wants to teach in high school. Richard is the most fun of all to be with but he lives only for today — has no ambition at all." I am not suggesting that many people make marital decisions based just on dollars and cents; I do think that consciously or unconsciously such matters do influence the marital selection process to some degree in a great number of cases. Finally, I think it is fair to say that the whole selection process is based on the hopes of maximizing the "for better" and minimizing the risk of "for worse" in marriage. That people do this is not unloving; it is to recognize that in marriage the couple will want as many things in their favor as possible, that love is more than mutual attraction to each other's face and figure. I think it is fair to say that most people do try to minimize the risk through various selection techniques before they enter into marriage.

To attempt to minimize the risk of marriage before entering into it is one thing. It would be something of an entirely different nature if the couple together (or either one separately) were to exclude positively the risk itself of marriage. For example, if a couple before marriage agreed that in the case of a crippling or debilitating sickness after marriage they would be "free agents" once again, or if they agreed to stick together as long as everything was working out satisfactorily but that they would be free agents once again if the union didn't work out — such a couple simply wouldn't be married no matter how grandiose the ceremony even if it were presided over by the Pope himself.[5] To the outside world, it may look like a marriage but it is not; it is only an agreement to co-habitate as long as the sun is shining, the roses are blooming, and the jasmine is filling the bedroom with perfume.

On the other hand, many couples and individuals, recognizing the difficulties of married life, try to reduce the risks not only through the selection process but also by postponement of marriage until they are able to accept the full responsibilities of marriage. This is not being inhuman or cold and calculating although it does involve the destruction of marriage seen as an idol to be worshipped as the panacea of everyone's personal problems. It is simply the recognition that the covenant of marriage involves far more than the expression of affective love and doing things together. It involves a recognition that it is sometimes good and even necessary to postpone the full union of the marital embrace in order to secure some of the other values associated with responsible marriage. Couples such as these try to minimize the risks in marriage in a responsible way without negating in any way the risk inherent in the faith commitment of marriage itself. Having attempted to be prudent in their planning and timing, they still enter into marriage knowing that the best laid plans of men often go astray and that their commitment is not based on their plans but exists rather in spite of the fact that their plans and hopes may fail.

Some couples may find that their socio-economic-educational backgrounds make it possible to eliminate almost completely the external risks to which any marriage is liable. Others may not even care about such matters; or if they do care, they may be unable to do as much as they would like about them. I would be the last one in the world to say that the marriage of a young couple who marry without any savings, income, education or job prospects but only a strong love for each other is any more — (or any less) — of a valid marriage than that of the couple which has such factors as material advantages. The point is that when the

---

5. Admittedly, *proving* such invalidity in the external forum to a marriage tribunal might be impossible.

people of either type of couple marry, they do so without reservation and recognize that any plans are subordinate to their marriage covenant.

(d) *Rhythm in Marriage.* By analogy, the couple who practice rhythm are like the couple who attempt to reduce the external risks of marriage not only by selection but also by the postponement of a marriage date until various conditions are more satisfactory. The couple practicing periodic continence or rhythm are likewise trying to reduce the risk of all the problems that they see associated with a pregnancy at this time by postponing the full sexual union as an expression of their love. They do not love each other less during the time of continence — any more so than they loved each other less during a chaste courtship. During the time of periodic continence they will have to show affection and love for each other in a manner akin to their chaste behavior before marriage. When they do choose to express their love and affection in the marital sex-union, they are hopeful that the consequences will be the same as they hoped for in their initial marriage covenant "for richer, in health, for better." They are hopeful that a pregnancy which they think will bring conditions of "for poorer, in sickness, for worse" will not occur. Nevertheless, by the fact that they are still only hopeful and have not positively excluded the risk element they still enter into a valid renewal of their original marriage covenant. There is still the risk of faith, the risk of covenant love, the risk of putting their lives in the hands of their Father-Creator.

The couple for whom periodic abstinence is an effective means of family planning are certainly in a more favored position than the couple who have much higher risks in this regard. I wish I had an easy answer for these latter couples.[6] Instead I can only answer that this must be seen in the light of all the other inequalities in life and marriage. Why one couple should

6. 1976: The natural family planning answer is more effective and thus "easier" than was realized when this was first written in 1970. See Appendix I.

have all the amenities of life while another struggles for existence leads to a discussion of the entire problem of evil, and such a discussion is not within the scope of this book. My present point is that the relative efficiency of periodic continence is analogous to the relative success of pre-marital plans or hopes to reduce the external risks of life together. Neither the presence nor the effectiveness of such plans vitiates the marriage covenant. However, if family planning within marriage takes on the proportions of an absolute so that it positively excludes the faith-risk inherent in the marriage act, then it invalidates such marriage acts and violates the marriage covenant.

In summary, it is not prior planning but only the absolutizing of the favorable "better" elements with the consequent positive exclusion of the negative elements involved in the marital risk of faith that vitiates the marriage covenant. Similarly, it is not family planning as such that vitiates the marriage act but only the absolutizing of the attractive unitive aspects with the consequent positive exclusion of the procreative elements involved in the marital embrace which is meant to be a renewal of the marriage covenant with its inherent risk of faith.

Both the original covenant and the sacramental renewal of it may be postponed. However, once the respective actions are no longer postponed but are realized, then the couple must be open to the faith-risk inherent in each.

4.   The Covenant Theology Applied to Other Sexual Activity

I have mentioned previously that a theory has increased value as it covers more and more cases. Because the covenant theory is simple, it will take but a short space to apply it to the areas of sexual activity that we have considered thus far. I think it will be seen that the theological statement agrees well with the common consent of mankind as found in our ordinary use of language.

(a) *"Loveless" Relations*. Rape is clearly a violation of the order of creation. The very word tells us that there is here no renewal of a marriage covenant. What about that form of sexual activity within marriage itself which is sometimes called "no better than rape?" I refer here to the case where the man demands his "marriage rights," where the wife consents out of fear for her bodily safety, or in those lesser cases where there is no love or affection between the couple but only a biological relation whereby the man can relieve himself of sexual tension. This covenant theology applies to these as well as to contraception. To the extent that the sexual relations between husband and wife are a *de facto* denial of the love, care, tenderness, faith, hope, risk and self-denial of the marriage covenant, to that extent they are non-authentic and even invalid. To spell it out more explicitly, this means that according to this theory, marital relations that are *opposed* to marital love are objectively sinful even though perhaps not defective from a biological point of view.

Prostitution is clearly outside the marriage covenant; so also is the more legitimized form of mistressing. So also is that form of "marriage" which is really no risk in faith covenant but a *de facto* arrangement for an exchange of bedding privileges for good support.

(b) *Pre- and Extra-Marital Relations.* Fornication and pre-marital relations likewise are clearly outside the marriage covenant; so is adultery. This is not to deny the very real personal affection and even love that may exist between people not married to each other whether still single or already married to someone else. It is not to deny the temporary relief of tension or the temporary sense of fulfillment gained by the parties to such actions. What I do deny is that these actions are authentic expressions of human love, for authentic love finds a valid full sexual expression only within the marriage covenant. One of the chief values of the covenant theory is its insistence on the inter-personal relationship without letting that fall into the fallacy of meaning that love is really a function of your intention. Many fornicators and adulterers feel, I am sure, that they are doing something loving; they may intend "love." I contend that their intention is insufficient because it does not match up with the objective criteria of the marriage covenant.

(c) *Sexual Perversions.* A more difficult area of sexual activity to account for under this theory is the realm of sexual perversion — masturbation, homosexuality, oral and anal intercourse. Sexual perversities are usually not the subject of polite conversation. Yet they have long been the subject of investigation by moralists and sexologists as well. The most famous of the latter was, of course, Sigmund Freud, though he was also much more than that. Reference to him will be useful for three reasons: (1) He openly advances a theoretical criteria by which sexual activity can be evaluated. (2) It may prove psychologically helpful for many to realize that one need not be a papalist to conclude that those forms of sexual activity which positively exclude the possibility of reproduction are perverse. (3) His testimony helps to answer the objection that only Catholics (and Orthodox and some Protestants) see anything wrong with contraception.

The quotations are from a series of lectures given by Freud in Vienna during the year 1917-1918.[7]

> . . . Our duty is to account satisfactorily in theory for the existence of all the perversions described and to explain their relation to normal sexuality, so called.
> . . . Such aberrations from the sexual aim, such erratic relationships to the sexual object, have been manifested since the beginning of time through every age of which we have knowledge, in every race from the most primitive to the most highly civilized, and at times have succeeded in attaining to toleration and general prevalance (p. 269).
> . . . Perverted sexuality is nothing else but infantile sexuality, magnified and separated into its component parts (p. 272).

---

7. Sigmund Freud, *A General Introduction to Psycho-Analysis,* translated by Joan Riviere (New York: Liverwright Publishing Co., 1935).

. . . for if a child has a sexual life at all, it must be of a perverted order, since apart from a few obscure indications he is lacking in all that transforms sexuality into the reproductive function. Moreover, it is a characteristic common to all the perversions that in them reproduction as an aim is put aside. This is actually the criterion by which we judge whether a sexual activity is perverse — if it departs from reproduction in its aims and pursues the attainment of gratification independently. You will understand therefore that the gulf and turning point in the development of the sexual life lies at the point of its subordination to the purposes of reproduction. Everything that occurs before this conversion takes place, and everything which refuses to conform to it and serves the pursuit of gratification alone is called by the unhonored title of "perversion" and as such is despised (p. 277).

Obviously Freud is condemning all those forms of sexual activity that do not result in human heterosexual copulation using the respective reproductive organs. He does not specifically mention contraception nor does he mention anal intercourse either. He contents himself to one criteria: the departure from reproduction in its aims and the pursuit of the attainment of gratification independently. Contraception was certainly practiced in Europe when Freud spoke; he could not have helped but know about it; yet he did not exclude it from his condemnation of perverse behavior.

Freud was certainly no papalist as is evident from his dismissal of conventional morality. Yet he saw that the reproductive purpose was so essential to human sexuality that he made its exclusion the criteria for evaluation of sexual perversion. Freud is a valuable witness, but I think that the covenant theory is a more valuable criteria for the evaluation of sexual behavior.

(d) *Masturbation.* To return to some evident aberrations, I think that masturbation is condemned by the covenant theory because it violates what is meant to be an interpersonal renewal of the covenant. Masturbation is a solitary act and has nothing to do with a renewal of the marriage covenant. Furthermore, that form of masturbation which some moralists want to say is not the human act of masturbation but the human act of obtaining semen for fertility analysis is also rejected by the covenant theory. This theory removes the sexual activity from the sole realm of the person's intention and asks if this is an interpersonal renewal of the covenant. Masturbation even for semen to be used to foster fertility is still the deliberate action of a human being who has de-personalized, de-humanized sexual activity which is meant to be solely an interpersonal expression of the marital covenant. It is no less against the order of creation than is artificial insemination. Both take an action meant to be interpersonal and make it only biological — despite any and all good intentions. As I have said before, sexual activity plays such an important role in the life of man that any deliberate sexual stimulation, and especially that culminating in orgasm, is a significant human act to be considered in itself and not just as part of a larger totality.

(e) *Homosexuality.* Homosexuality is definitely interpersonal activity. Some homosexuals "marry" and tend to remain "faithful" to each other, are not promiscuous, and consider themselves to be living a "higher life," one which certainly does not burden the world with more mouths to feed. They do not consider their behavior as "selfish" nor do they consider that they are doing something which is "un-natural" for them. They may regard normal heterosexual activity as "un-natural" for themselves.

The normal heterosexual would do well not to look down his nose at these people. I am not condoning homosexuality, but if there is anyone for whom I feel sorry in the entire modern sexual problem it is the person with homosexual tendencies who does not want to become a practicing homosexual. A person like this called me on the phone to ask if I did any counseling. We got talking and he said he was what people called "a queer." He wasn't giving in to his tendencies; he was going to Mass and receiving the sacraments regularly, but he felt completely left out of society. The whole society, even Church groups, seemed oriented to the couple — already existing or matchmaking. Where was there a place for him who had no interest in matchmaking but did need honest companionship? My sympathies extend to this young man in a way that they do not to the contraceptive couple — even that couple whose family situation calls for heroism of a sort. The married couple — even if living as brother and sister — still have each other, and that was supposed to mean a lot before they got married. They may feel constrained not to have a sexual union, and they may find this extremely difficult — but at least they have a union of mind and heart. They have the psychological fulfillment of knowing that they are fully accepted by the other, loved by the other, and are being helped by the other on the path of salvation.

The genetic or psychological homosexual who refuses to become a practicing homosexual has no one. His is the loneliest life of all, and my heart aches for those unknown homosexuals who are bravely fighting a terrific battle, alone except for their confessor and their Faith. However, at the same time, it must be admitted that the genetic/psychological homosexual's plight of loneliness is probably no worse than that of many a normal heterosexual who longs for the companionship and acceptance by someone of the opposite sex but cannot find it for one reason or another.

But what about the interpersonal practice of homosexuality? Where does it stand in a theory which works from a personalist and sacramental starting point? If the theory was based solely on personal intentions of affection and commitment, it would seem that a homosexual "marriage," if such really ever occurred, would be a valid covenant and homosexual relations would be a valid renewal of that covenant.

However, the covenant is theologically based first and foremost on the free and personal agreement to enter not just a covenant of the couple's own making, but the covenant of marriage which is a God-given relationship. It is a relationship which has an order intended by the Creator, a structure which is not dependent solely upon the intentions of the two people.

The question then arises, "How can you be sure that this structure, this order of Creation, does not include homosexual marriages?" As stated previously, we are always somewhat limited regarding "proofs" in the area of human life. When dealing with human behavior, we never get the sort of mathematical proof that we can have about the statement "sixteen divided by eight equals two." In human behavior we can strive only for moral certitude when we work from reason alone. This is the kind of certitude we have for making all the big decisions in life, such as deciding that you love this particular person and want to marry. As an example, try this: Imagine you are talking with a skeptic who says he doesn't think you really love your spouse. Try to prove it to him. If the skeptic has any sort of imagination at all, he will be able to answer anything you advance. Finally, you will be driven to conclude that he is just being absurd to deny all the practical evidence, but this still doesn't amount to mathematical certitude. What you have arrived at, however, is a moral certitude that you love your spouse.

In answering that an interpersonal relationship of fidelity, care, and affection between two homosexuals cannot be the structure of marriage, I would point first of all to the common consent of mankind that marriage takes place only between people of the opposite sex. I think we can say without fear of contradiction that homosexuality has always been regarded as an abnormality, no matter how widely practiced.

Secondly, I would enlist the service of Freud who taught, as we have seen, that the criteria for judging the perversity of a sexual act was whether or not it departed from reproduction in its aims and purposes. As some New York homosexuals have recently argued, their way of life certainly is one answer to the problem of the population explosion. It will never be reproductive, and so, according to Freud, it is perverse.

Thirdly, I would call attention to the long history of a natural law tradition which has pointed out very well that man's and woman's sexual organs complement each other; one is made for the other; and only through normal heterosexual activity can reproduction occur. (I pass over artificial insemination). The sexual power is oriented to reproduction at all levels of life. The fact that man can use his sexual power just for personal enjoyment to the positive exclusion of any possibility of reproduction is a sociological fact but still does not deny the natural, normative orientation of sexual activity towards reproduction. It is God, not the Pope, who has joined the unitive and procreative aspects of sexual intercourse.

I think it is worthwhile to note that this covenant theology does not contradict the natural law tradition which has been biologically oriented. At times it is necessary to look at the physiology of man, for man is not just spirit and intentions but matter and physiology as well. I think it is an advantage of this covenant theology that it can still make use of this natural law tradition. The covenant theory does not exclude but rather subsumes the values and many of the arguments of the natural law tradition. I consider it a higher-level theory because it can answer more problems in a more completely human way, but it does not simply do away with as irrelevant the tradition of the past.

Fourthly, there is the Judeo-Christian tradition contained in the Scriptures condemning homosexuality. This may seem in the eyes of the believer to be the most powerful argument, and perhaps it is. However, I refrain from depending on it exclusively simply because any argument based on Scripture may be quickly shot down by the simple method of interpretation. For example, the judgment on the homosexuals of Sodom could be advanced as a biblical teaching that homosexuality is evil. However, someone is sure to come along and say that it wasn't homosexuality as such that was condemned but only the inhospitality of the Sodomites. Again, St. Paul's condemnation of men entering into unnatural relations with men would seem a very strong argument (Rom 1). However, it is no trick to take the bite out of that simply by asserting that St. Paul was condemning only *promiscuous* homosexuality — and that he was influenced by Stoicism, etc. It is important to remember that if Scripture contained the statement, "Thou shalt not contracept under any circumstances," one could easily take the teeth out of that by saying that the sacred author was referring to specific circumstances of which he was aware *at the time*. A Scripture passage really gets its teeth only from the use of it by the Church in its teaching. In this latter case we can rely on our faith that the Holy Spirit, the guiding author of Scripture also guides the Church in its ordinary teaching as well as in its extraordinary *ex cathedra* definitions.

I think that by stressing that sexual relations are meant to be a renewal of the covenant of marriage, and by stressing that the marriage covenant is meant to be heterosexual, homosexuality of even the most refined sort is seen to be a violation of the order of creation.

(f) *Oral and Anal Intercourse.* It is difficult to write about oral and anal intercourse. I suspect that some readers will not have known previously that people, especially married people, even did such things. Unfortunately some people do.

The minority report of the papal birth control commission pointed out that the majority position was open to the practice of anal and oral intercourse. The majority never really answered the objection in an adequate way but only with a gratuitous assertion that they condemned these forms of sexual activity and that, in these acts, neither the dignity of love nor the dignity of the spouses was preserved. This is basically an argument from their own authority; no reasons are given to explain on what grounds they based their condemnation.

I mentioned this one day to a priest who had subscribed to the contraception argument. His answer was quite frank: maybe we should just stop worrying about such things and admit that within marriage "anything goes."

The brutal fact of the matter is that a theory of sex which is a *de facto* theory of personal intentionalism simply has no answer to either homosexuality or anal/oral intercourse. If the important criteria of the sexual act is the expression of "personal love" and this particular couple feels that they can best express their personal affective love, their willingness to give of each to the other through oral or anal intercourse, on what basis can this behavior be condemned? On a radical personalist basis, is it not really true that "anything goes?" The couple are not consciously being selfish, they are not consciously exploiting each other, they are just being their naturally-loving personal selves, contributing to the widening experience and development of each other. If there were a taboo on oral and anal intercourse, wouldn't this interfere with the natural spontaneity of sexual expression, an interference so criticized by some of the personalist advocates of contraception?

The covenant theory can have a strong personalist attitude and yet escape the weaknesses of radical personalism (*de facto* intentionalism) because it stresses first of all the God-given structure of marriage. It states that marriage is first of all heterosexual; then that the heterosexual structure is oriented both to the mutual development of love and to new life; then that the personalist aspect may not positively exclude the reproductive aspect, the risk element. It can then condemn oral and anal intercourse because they are *de facto* positive exclusions of any possibility of the reproductive, risk element. Furthermore, since the covenant theory does not exclude but rather subsumes the natural law tradition it can argue along the Freudian line that sexual behavior is perverse to the extent that it departs from reproduction in its aims and purposes. As a minimal interpretation of Freud, it is clear that he regards as perverse all mutual sex activity which is not at least mutually genital. I agree. The sex organs are made for each other; they are organs of reproduction as well as of love; to use them as love organs while positively excluding the reproductive aspect through oral/anal intercourse is a violation of the interpersonal order of the created covenant.

5.   A Corollary

In the past several pages dealing with the manner of evaluating perversities, I have drawn attention to the fact that the covenant theory and the natural law tradition do not contradict each other but that the covenant theory is related to the natural law theory as the general to the more specific, a higher level to a lower one. Now it seems that I must part company with the natural law theory as understood in an exclusively biological sense, or at least as I understand it in that way. I want to treat the problem of contraception outside of the marital embrace.

It seems to me that the traditional natural law theory centers the evil of contraception on a biological interference which positively prevents a union of sperm and ova. It seems to me that such an approach does not make adequate provision for the difference between marital and non-marital sexual intercourse. The strictly biological approach seems to say that contraception adds additional immorality or unnaturality to sexual relations which are already illicit. It seems to say that the prostitute somehow sins twice if she uses contraceptives to avoid pregnancy.

Here I think it is extremely important to note the distinction between the teaching of the Catholic Church and the older theories advanced in support of that teaching. The older natural law would indicate that the Church should teach that contraception was immoral for adulterers, prostitutes, etc. In fact, however, the official teaching of the Church as represented by *Casti Connubii* (1931) and *Humanae Vitae* (1968) limits its prohibition of contraception to the *marital embrace*. These encyclicals simply avoid the question about the morality of contraception for the unmarried. It is my opinion that a theory of natural law which centers too much on the strictly biological has not afforded sufficient latitude to account for the difference between contraception in the marital embrace and contraception in a non-marital union.

This covenant theology says that the biological act of contraception is wrong not just because it interferes with the biological process of transmitting life but rather because such physical interference is the concrete *sign* of the refusal of the married couple to let this sexual union be an authentic renewal of their marriage covenant. Their unwillingness to accept the covenantal consequences is "incarnated" in the process of contraception.

But what about those sexual unions which are already a violation of the order of creation because they are outside the covenant of marriage? I cannot help but conclude that in these cases contraception is a valid sign of the reality that there is no willingness, right, or obligation to be open to the risk of supporting new life and growing in love as a result. I have said that contraception is evil because it violates the interpersonal order of a marriage covenant created by God and entered into by this couple. Where there is no covenant, it seems to me that there is no evil to contraception.

Non-marital sex acts are already a *de facto* dishonesty. They pretend to be a sign of self-giving love but they are not, despite the best intentions. Contraception is a sign of this dishonesty, this going through the motions without either a valid covenant or a valid renewal of that covenant. Contraception becomes honest only when it is admitted to be a sign of an already existing dishonesty.

In terms of the unitive-procreative aspects of sexual intercourse, we can say that since there is no valid unitive aspect present in sexual relations outside of a true marriage bond, there should be no procreative aspect either.

I am not advocating that the unmarried male carry contraceptives in his wallet in imitation of the famous Boy Scout motto, "Be prepared." In my opinion, by such preparedness he has already consented to fornication. The same holds true for single girls who would take contraceptives as sort of a general precaution. Nor am I advocating any sort of pre-marital relations, either with or without contraceptives. I am only saying that where the sexual relations are already immoral, already dishonest because they do not renew an existing marriage covenant, then contraception adds no additional infraction of the order of creation but is simply a sign of the dishonesty of those relations.

I think that this theorizing is in full accord with the explicit teaching of the Church and that it shows the advantage of the structural covenant theory over a theory of natural law that is concerned with the biological processes in themselves rather than as a sign of the interpersonal relationship.

6.   A Few Questions

In the review of this chapter, it occurred to me that various comments might be made from both the left, middle, and right in the contraception controversy. It would have been possible to incorporate these in the main text, but it seemed that the purpose of clarity and brevity might be better served by treating them separately.

(1) *Question*: *To what extent is this theory biblical?*

Response: It is biblical first of all in the broad sense of being a form of covenant theology. The covenant is perhaps the most basic theme in the Bible. It is biblical in the second place because it allows for an interpretation of Genesis 38:10 that sees here the sin of contraception as a sin against a covenant. As indicated previously, Onan was not the only one to violate the Law of the Levirate in this specific situation, for his father and younger brother also disobeyed it by default. However, Onan engaged in the act called for by the Levirate "covenant" but contradicted it. The sin for which the Sacred authors tell us he was punished was not the violation of the Levirate which he would have violated if he had merely refused to have intercourse with Tamar; rather it was his participation in the covenanted act and his contraceptive invalidation of it that was so sinful that he was punished while the others in his family were not.

The covenant theory is not opposed to St. Paul's self-styled concession to married people about not refusing each other except perhaps for a while by mutual agreement lest they be tempted by lack of self-control (1 Cor 7:3-6). Whether the abstinence be for prayer or more secular values, the covenant theory merely states that when they do come together again it be a valid renewal of the marriage covenant.

It is, of course, in accord with the further Pauline teaching in Ephesians 5 where the self-sacrificing love of Christ for his Church is held up as the model for a husband's love for his wife. The new covenant was made in the blood of Christ shed for his Church for its holiness, and this covenant theology calls for a somewhat analogous death to self in order to promote the holiness of each marriage. The union of Christ and his Church is described by St. Paul as a mystery; so is the marriage covenant.

Finally the theory is biblical in the sense that it calls for those values and attitudes which are specifically and habitually rejected by the world — a radical teaching on fidelity to the marriage covenant, an attitude of denial of self and trusting surrender in Christ, and an attitude toward material goods that tends to place one among the Bible's *anawim* rather than among society's *beautiful people.*

(2) *Question*: Is it possible that the use of the phrase "order of creation" instead of "natural law" may lead some to rationalize that the order of creation in their circumstances is so out of order that they are justified in using contraception?

Response: Yes. Such rationalization isn't justified or implicit in this theory, but that is no guarantee it won't take place. However, I think that such a situation would be preferable to the present rationale that is used to justify contraception. At the present, people are dismissing the Church's teaching as erroneous or irrelevant and tend to lose faith in the Church's teaching authority in all areas of moral life. A process of rationalization as envisioned in the question would at least (1) keep faith in the Church as an authoritative moral teacher, (2) make the couple realize that they are trying to counter one evil with another, (3) make the couple realize that their solution of one evil to counteract another tends to provide the rationalization for adultery, fornication and every other violation of the sexual order of creation as well as for just about every sin imaginable.

(3) *Question*: Does the sacramental approach of this theology depart from the traditional teaching that contraception violates the natural law?

Response: No, but it does approach the meaning of the natural law from a different perspective. It takes the position that the natural law for man is to be found more in an interpersonal analysis than in a biological one. This approach states that man has the freedom to commit himself and to covenant himself in such a way that certain physical actions subsequently become immoral. It states that it is against the nature of being human to marry one person and to sleep with another. At the same time, it is free to admit that many human beings act contrary to the nature of being fully human and consider themselves to be doing what comes naturally. It further recognizes the very real limits of any natural law theory and the indispensable source we have in Jesus Christ — God become man to teach us what it means for us to become authentically human.

(4) *Question*: Won't this theology be unacceptable to modern man if for no other reason than that it takes contraception out of the realm of individual conscience and makes it a matter of universal negative?

Response: According to this theology, contraception is no more and no less a matter of personal conscience than are other areas of sexual behavior. If some people today will not accept a universal negative with regard to adultery or fornication, they will not accept such a statement about contraception either. If they accept universal negatives in other areas of sexual behavior, they should logically be willing to accept it with regard to contraception. Finally, the search for what is objectively true about love in this regard should not be impeded by the appeal to individual conscience. The purpose of the authoritative moral teaching of the Church is to provide a sure norm for the formation of conscience. The purpose of this theory is to show that the Church's authoritative moral teaching about contraception is true and consistent with its teaching about marriage itself.

(5) *Question*: Does this theology take adequate account of the very real hardships of many couples including the difficulty inherent in prolonged abstinence?

Response: It shares this painful difficulty with the traditional Catholic teaching about the indissoluble character of the marriage bond. The agonizing situation of some persons who are involved in truly valid Christian marriages had lead some theologians to talk about spiritually dead marriages as no longer binding. (That such theologizing comes in the face of the solid Scriptural foundation for Catholic doctrine in this regard and that it is somewhat simultaneous with the efforts to change the doctrine of non-contraception lends credence to the belief that both efforts are more the product of the sexual mores of the day than the message of the gospel.) In the face of excruciating problems in both cases I can only say that if I had to pick my agony, I would pick the problems stemming from non-contraception rather than those stemming from indissolubility. I'd much prefer that companionship (without sexual intercourse) of a loving wife to the loneliness of a person whose valid Christian marriage status is that of one deserted or divorced.

(6) *Question*: Does this theory about individual acts lead to the conclusion that a couple who keep individual acts open to the faith-risk of the covenant but strive through periodic abstinence never to have any children for a serious reason are leading an authentic Christian marriage?

Response: It doesn't say anything specific about this. It is in full accord with the doctrine of Vatican II about fostering the nobility of marriage and the family (*The Church in the Modern World,* Part II, Chapter 1).

(7) *Question*: Does this theory prove conclusively that the biological act of contraception is immoral?

Response: This theory has not proved or attempted to prove that the biological act of contraception is immoral. Rather it has openly stated that the biological act of contraception is not immoral for persons not validly married to each other. It has stated that the immorality of contraception within an authentic marriage is that it is a concrete sign of a refusal to renew the marriage covenant in the marital act which is meant-to-be such a renewal of covenant love. As an aside, I might add that this theory would of course see no difficulty in giving any sort of contraceptive to anyone in danger of rape.

(8) *Question*: Since the element of risk figures in this theology, what is the difference between the risk of the rhythm method

and the risk of a contraceptive known to be less than 100% effective in practice?

Response: The difference lies not just in statistical or material differences, but in the difference between essential and accidental, formal and material. The couple practicing rhythm consciously leave the marriage act — when they enter that communion — open to the faith-risk of covenant love. Their communion is essentially open to both the better and the worse of their covenant. The couple practicing contraception consciously have closed each and every contraceptive marriage act to the faith-risk of covenant love. Their communion is essentially closed to the element of worse in the covenant although chemical and mechanical imperfections may render it accidentally open to life. In terms of formal and material, the practice of rhythm is both formally and materially open to the faith-risk of the marital covenant; the practice of contraception is formally and materially closed to it. If a particular contraceptive act should happen to be open to life, it would only be open to life by accident and would still be contrary to the formality of the contraceptive act.

Some examples serve to highlight the difference. Two persons, A and B, have had a strong conflict. A decides to avoid B in order to remove the possibility of future conflict. However, A resolves, if and when they meet, he will be open to B and do nothing to harm him. B on the contrary decides to seek out A and to kill him. He finds A, shoots, but only manages to wound him. He flees undetected and later repents, deciding to do what he can to help A. B was at first essentially closed to the life of A. His openness to the life of A was strictly *per accidens* even though he later decided to cherish that life.

I do not doubt that many couples who practice contraception will not resort to abortion even when it is readily available although this has become the pattern in countries where contraception is the rule of life and abortion is merely considered part of the package to back up its failures. One can be closed to the renewal of the marriage covenant and all that it entails and still be open to the more basic "covenant of life" which exists among all living human beings.

Another example: A couple agrees before marriage that the union will be dissolved in the face of certain unfortunate events. Some years later one of these events occurs. Upon further consideration, they decide to stick together. They were formally and essentially closed to the marriage covenant. From their reaction to the event, it would seem that they were open *per accidens* to some of the risk, but in this example we still do not have them committing themselves to be faithful in the face of all future adversities.

A third consideration: From an existential point of view at the present time, there is certainly a difference between those Catholics who refrain from contraception as part of their religious commitment and those who practice it in the face of authoritative teaching to the contrary. It amounts to a difference in what is willed primarily and secondarily. The couple who practice rhythm are primarily willing to be faithful to their marriage covenant as explicated by the Church and only secondarily will and hope to avoid conception. The couple who practice contraception directly and primarily will to avoid conception and secondarily will to contravene the moral teaching of the Church.

(9) *Question*: Doesn't this theology make risk rather than love the basis of marriage?

Response: Early in this chapter, I expressed my conviction that the word "love" has become an almost meaningless term because it is used by so many different people to mean so many different things. In the development of the covenant theology of marriage, I tried to show that one of the essential components of marital love is the acceptance of the faith-risk of the marital covenant. In terms of the historic People of God, their acceptance of the faith-risk of their Covenant was to be and still is a sign of their love for God. The same is true of the marital covenant. In both, love is signified by the risk of faith and fidelity; in both covenants, faith-risk and love cannot be divorced, nor can one substitute for the other. Love remains the basis of both covenants, and in both love is much more than feeling.

Chapter Six

HOLY COMMUNION: REVEALED, EUCHARISTIC

AND MARITAL [1]

If a theory developed for one particular area of human behavior cannot be applied to other areas of human life and values
without creating havoc, it should be apparent that the theory is
erroneous. On the contrary, if a theory which explains one area
of human behavior can be applied to other areas of human
life and values, and by that process becomes all the more meaningful, then the value of that theory is increased. A failure to fit
in with the larger scope of reality does not *automatically disprove*
the new theory; it is theoretically possible that the theory is right
and the understanding of the rest of reality is in error. Nor does
the fittingness of the new theory with the understanding of the
rest of reality *automatically prove* its rightness. Theoretically,
both could be erroneous, or the fittingness might be just happen-
stance. Nevertheless, the more the new theory fits in with and
gives additional meaning to other aspects of reality, the more
weight it must normally carry. When certain aspects of the rest of
reality are known with the infallible certainty of faith or are known
with a high degree of theological certainty, a theory which fits in
well with these certainties becomes more certain also.

I believe that such is the case with the covenant theory of
sexual relations. First of all, it can be seen as an extension of the

---

1. Much of this chapter first appeared as "Holy Communion, Eucharistic
and Marital," *Ave Maria*, February 27, 1967.

covenant communion between God and man which is at the heart of biblical religion.[2] Then it can be seen as especially adaptable to and parallel with the covenant of the Eucharistic communion.

1. Revelation

One does not have to be a student of the Bible to realize that the Judeo-Christian religion is built around a Covenant. Every Catholic who keeps his ears open at the Consecration of the Mass hears the words, "This is the chalice of my blood, of the new and everlasting Covenant." Even if he has never opened the Old Testament, he can pretty well figure out that if the Last Supper was concerned with the inauguration of the New Covenant, then the Jews were a people of a previous one which we today call the Old Covenant.

The covenant in the Old Testament can be traced back to Abram, the subject of a promissory covenant by God who said that he would make Abram the father of a great people even though he and Sarai were advanced in age and childless. Abram believed, left everything to walk with God, and put his fertility problem in the hands of God. This latter was probably the most difficult. Abram thought that his heir would be Eliezer, his household slave (Gen 15:3) but at the word of Yahweh he believed that it would be his own son. This belief is interpreted by St. Paul as being Abram's justification.

However, as Sarai did not become pregnant, it became problematic as to how Yahweh's promise of offspring would be fulfilled. Sarai took the initiative and followed the custom of the times: she provided Abram with a substitute to conceive a child over whom Sarai would hold all legal right. Abram pleaded that his son, Ishmael, might be his rightful heir, but Yahweh called for more faith and changed the names of Abram and Sarai to

---

2. For a detailed analysis of the Scriptural basis for this statement see Wilfrid J. Harrington, O.P., *The Promise To Love* (Staten Island, N.Y.: Alba House, 1968), p. 62.

Abraham and Sarah to denote their parenthood. Shortly thereafter, Sarah conceived and bore Isaac.

If one thing seems clear from this account it is that the sacred author is telling us that the covenant beginnings were intimately connected with the infertility problem of Abraham and Sarah and that Abraham was continually asked to put his faith in Yahweh. His greatness is that he was repeatedly willing to believe although the practical problems seemed insurmountable. His communion with Yahweh was one of faith, trust and a commitment to walk with God without reservation.

The covenant with the people through Moses was no less demanding but it was more explicit both in its recognition of Yahweh as their Savior and in its recognition of each other as brothers. The heart of the Covenant was its statement that Yahweh had saved the people and that to enjoy his blessings the people must act like his people. They must be faithful to him in worship; they must be faithful to him in their treatment of their fellow man; they must have trusting faith that he will deliver them from their enemies as he had done before. The sinfulness of the people is shown to be their infidelity to Yahweh in worship, their inhumanity to their fellow man, and their eagerness to play politics in order to avoid having to put their faith in Yahweh.

The covenant called for an interpersonal communion of the people with Yahweh. To be in communion with him, it was not sufficient just to recall what he had done. It was grossly insufficient to go through the motions of religious sacrifice. The religious sacrifice, even that which stemmed from the covenant itself, was an abomination if the external motions were not a faithful representation of one's internal communion with Yahweh. If the people were unwilling to be faithful to Yahweh, if they were unwilling to practice justice and righteousness, unwilling to trust in him alone as Deliverer and Savior, then they were not in the communion of the covenant, no matter how many of the covenant rituals they performed.

Jesus came not to destroy but to fulfill. He did not eliminate the spirit of the Old Covenant but taught us more clearly what it meant. To accept the Fatherhood of God meant to love one's neighbor. One's neighbor is everyone. He taught us that there are not really two great commands; one, to love God; the other, to love our neighbor. He taught instead that the two are really one: only by loving our neighbor do we really love God.

In Jesus we see the fulfillment of the covenant. He looked constantly to his Father in heaven, he lived out a life of justice and righteousness; he placed his fate entirely in the hands of his Father, even unto death.

In making a new "blood covenant" with his followers he left them with a ceremony by which they could both signify their communion with him and receive the strength necessary to live up to the covenant in his body and blood. It is completely inadequate to describe the Eucharistic Sacrifice as a ceremony, but there is always the danger that it can degenerate into that on the part of those participating in its celebration.

Here we must be very clear. The Mass, the Eucharistic Sacrifice, always has its saving character as a re-enactment, a re-living of the Last Supper. Christ, through his priest, always and infallibly continues his sacrifice on behalf of man in this sacramental manner. My interest, however, at this time is not to discuss the intrinsic value of the Mass or the Sacrament of the Eucharist. It is rather to look into the dispositions necessary for an authentic communion with Christ in his covenant with man. What does it mean to participate in and to renew the blood covenant with Christ?

It means first of all to walk with God in the faith of Abraham. There must be on the part of the Christian, no less than with Abraham, that willingness to put his fate into the hands of the Father despite apparently insurmountable obstacles.

It means to accept Jesus as the norm for our actions. To be in communion with him means to be in union with the mind and heart, the faith and hope and the sacrificial disposition of Christ at the Last Supper. To be in communion with Christ means to be with him all the way. It means at the very minimum not to be holding back deliberately, not to be going through the motions while in the heart there is a serious reservation.

Now, what has all this to do with marital communion and contraception? Just this: I think that an examination of the interpersonal communion of the covenant supports the theory that contraception is evil because it is a sign of a contradiction of the marriage covenant.

With regard to the spirit of the Old Covenant which is carried on into the New, contraception is a sign of unwillingness to accept the risk of faith; it is a sign of trust in science rather than a trust in Yahweh whose love is a demanding love. Contraception is a sign of faith in the prudence of men who can see only the insurmountable obstacles; it is an effective denial of faith in the prophetic voice which says that somehow God will bring good out of the problem if you act in true faith, if you really put your trust in him — but that this trust may well involve further suffering.

In examining the relationship between the marital covenant and the New Covenant, I will try to show that there is a basic similarity or sacramental identity between the Eucharistic and marital communion.

2.   Sacrament

Both the Eucharistic and the marital communions are sacramental actions. In the Eucharist we have the full sacrament renewed at each Eucharistic sacrifice. The bread and wine become the Body and Blood of Christ. In ordinary language we refer to the sacrament as the Eucharist when referring to the Body and Blood of Christ under the signs or appearances of bread and wine. However, when we speak of the action of the believer receiving the Eucharist, we tend to speak of Holy Communion. It is a communing action designed to make man holy. This action on the part of the individual believer is, in a sense, a sacramental action, for his personal action also has a sign value. It is a sign of his faith, a sign of his desire to be one with Christ, a sign of his desire to be nourished by this sacrament so that he can live up to the demands of the New Covenant. We can say that there is a twofold sign value in the Eucharistic communion.

There is the sign of Christ's nourishing, life-giving presence under the Eucharistic signs of bread and wine; there is the sign of the believer's desire to walk with Christ in his covenant.

The marital communion is likewise a sacramental action. To be theologically accurate, we should remember that the sacrament of Matrimony is conferred by the couple on each other only once just as we must remember that the sacrifice of the Last Supper and Calvary took place only once in the historic life of Jesus. Perhaps we should say that both Eucharistic and marital communions are the result of Sacraments. However, I think it is permissible and not misleading to speak of the marital communion as a sacramental action because it is meant to renew the original marriage covenant. It is an action that should take place only as a result of the marriage covenant between this man and this woman. As a sacramental action, it also has a sign value. It signifies the renewal of their mutual covenant with all that this entails.

I think that the importance of seeing the marital union as a sacramental action cannot be over-emphasized. I have mentioned earlier that a leading theory advanced by the contraceptionists is that it is sufficient for a holy marriage if the marriage as a whole is open to life, but that it is not necessary for each sexual union to be so. This is advanced as a legitimate extension of the principle of totality. I have already mentioned that Pope Paul VI disclaimed this as a valid application of the principle, and I have given my own reasons for thinking it invalid. If the married sexual union is accepted as a sacramental act, then the significance of each individual act becomes more apparent.

The sacramental theology of today is trying to maintain a a balance between what Christ does in the sacrament and what the person must do to benefit from the work of Christ. In the past, Catholic theology placed such emphasis on the work of Christ that the believer could easily misunderstand the sacramental encounter as something that would automatically make him "holy." The Catholic emphasis was partly a reaction against a Protestant one on the faith of the believer as being the real, and (seemingly) only cause of holiness in the sacramental encounter.

The current emphasis on the personal dispositions of the believer is necessary to maintain the typical Christian tension of "both . . . and" — *both* the work of Christ *and* the work of the believer, the work of Christ not "automatically" creating holiness, the dispositions of the believer not creative of the sacrament.

The person who is about to receive Holy Communion knows that he has to be open to Christ in order to receive what Christ wants to give him in this sacramental encounter. His openness will vary, his love will vary, his conscious reflection on the importance of what he is doing will vary. However, he knows that he may not vary to the extent of positively excluding part of his covenant commitment with Christ. That is, if he is turned away from God, if he is in a state of serious sin, if he is thus out-of-communion with God, he is not morally free to receive the Eucharist. For him to go through the motions which are a sign of communion when in his heart he is opposed to a real communion in the practical order is simply sacriligious.

To keep the tension of "both — and" in balance, it should be remembered that when a person sins, when he sets himself against God, it is rarely if ever by saying in so many words, "I will not serve . . . I hereby say 'No' to God." The axiom about actions speaking louder than words is extremely relevant here, as is the teaching of Christ, "You are my friends, if you do what I command you" (Jn 15:14). It is through refusal to keep the command that one says "No" to God, not by direct address. Certainly this is also the message of Matthew's last judgment scene.

The believer knows that in his sacramental life he cannot apply the principle of totality in a broad brush way (though a confessor may advise him to use it in solving a particular problem of conscience concerning whether he had sinned or not.) He cannot say, "Most of my life I've been for Christ. I've done what he commanded. Right now at this stage in my life I just don't buy it, but on the basis of my past and on what I hope for in the future when the present temptation is over, I'll receive the Eucharist." No, what is all important is not the past, be it good or bad, not the future hopes, but the "now." Each communion, even if it be so often as once a day, is a sacred reality and must be lived as such.

The marital communion is likewise a sacramental action. Its frequency does not detract from its unique reality. The couple may vary in their openness to each other and to God, their love will vary, their consciousness of the religious significance of their action may be completely missing. But at least one thing is necessary: there can be no real contradiction of their marriage covenant, there can be no action which is a *de facto* positive exclusion of willingness to walk with each other and with God in the risk of marriage and faith.

Just as man's covenant and communion with God is not broken just by the formal statement of "No" to God, so also the marriage covenant is not violated just by a formal "No" to each other or to God. In both cases, the actions speak louder than the words. Concrete refusal to help a neighbor who is calling for the help you can provide is a "No" to God, no matter how many times you say "God bless you." Concrete, positive contraception is a "No" to the faith and risk commitment of the marriage covenant no matter how many times the couple repeat their marriage vows and say "I love you." As in the Eucharistic communion, the interpersonal communion of the marital embrace is a sacred reality. Each act is a sacramental act and cannot be disregarded or subsumed under a broad brush application of totality.

The sacramental theology of marriage must maintain the dynamic Christian tension of "both — and." There is tremendous pressure today to place almost complete emphasis on the personalist side, the intentions of the couple, their overall disposition toward life and each other. To maintain the tension and the truth of the sacramental encounter it is necessary to remember that the actions themselves have a certain structure, a certain ability to say "Yes" or "No" to God and his covenant regardless of the intentions of the couple. It is also extremely necessary to remember that just as the Eucharistic communion does not auto-matically create a state of increased holiness within the believer, neither does the marital communion in any way automatically create a state of increased holiness within the couple or in any way automatically create the couple as more loving persons. In the Eucharist, growth is contingent upon openness to the risk of walking the narrow way with Christ; so also in the marriage em-brace, growth in love is contingent upon openness to the risk of the marriage covenant.

I would not want to leave the impression that I think that non-contraception is the only factor in the value of the married sex act. I believe that within marriage itself there is a range of value roughly corresponding to the range outside of marriage. At the low end of the scale there is the intercourse which is devoid of affection and consideration. It is not even a considerate seeking of relief from sexual tension; in some literature it is termed rape. Such an action is hardly in keeping with the marriage cove-nant; there is no interpersonal communion; it is invalid. Within the range of the acceptable, the same couple may have relations which are simply enjoyable, pleasurable sex play, or are a culmination of a felt personal union which had been shown by repeated acts of consideration and kindness all during the day or week. I would put at the top of the value range that act which is a real inter-personal communion in which the couple consciously desire their love to be personified in the new life of a third person. It seems to me that in this moment they reflect the love of the Trinity, the mutual love of the Father and the Son which is personified in the Holy Spirit.

Some of the personalist theologizing on marriage has left me uneasy. When I hear of a theologian telling students that at the moment of orgasm the floodgates of sanctifying grace are opened, I find it hard to go along for many reasons. Some of this writing almost encourages a new form of scrupulosity or self-deception: it makes it appear that only that sexual intercourse is valid which is a culmination of tremendous love, whatever love is. The poor couple who simply feel like having sex, without worrying about how loving they are, seem to be either left out, called immoral, led to a new scrupulosity, or driven to calling their every sex act a fantastic act of love which is probably intellectual dishonesty.

I think that the contraceptive and the rape-type acts are invalid as an expression of marital love but that within the area of the acceptable there is quite a range of degrees of love, just as there is with the Eucharistic communion. I believe that most (or at least many) couples can analyze their marital relations and find room for making them more expressive of the love of the Christian marriage covenant.

3.   The Covenant

A problem that concerns Catholics and others who believe in infant baptism has to do with the fact that there is no personal commitment on the part of the infant when he is baptized. He is brought into the life of the Church as an adopted son of God, but when does he ever personalize the commitment made on his behalf by his godparents?

His baptism, however, looks forward to his First Holy Communion. The Eucharist, as it were, signs or seals the covenant entered upon at baptism. It is a renewal of the baptismal covenant. Perhaps it might be said better that baptism introduces us to the covenant made at the Last Supper and through our celebration of the Eucharist we can renew that covenant. At any rate, there is a most intimate connection between baptism and the Eucharist, and that connection is found in the covenant. When the believer celebrates the Eucharist and receives Holy Communion he has the opportunity of pledging his fidelity once again to Christ in the New Covenant. He has the opportunity of personalizing his commitment. When he says "Amen" he can be saying "I'm with you, Jesus, all the way, for better *and* for worse." I would not venture to say that these are the conscious thoughts of any one or all believers who receive Holy Communion. However, I remain convinced that the Communion will be holy to the extent that the person is open to the demands of the covenant and that the liturgical ceremony should assist the faithful to arrive at this inner spirit of oneness with Christ and the Church at the Last Supper.

As has been mentioned repeatedly, the marital communion is likewise a renewal of the marriage covenant. It provides the opportunity for the couple to renew the faith and love which they first expressed at their wedding. How many couples make any conscious connection between their sexual relations and the covenant relationship of their wedding day is unknown. The validity of the theory does not rest on a sociological survey anymore than the validity of calling the Eucharistic communion a renewal of the Last Supper covenant rests upon such a survey. I am of the opinion that in our educational process we should help people to realize the covenantal relationships in both communions, Eucharistic and marital.

The aspect of covenant also offers an answer to one of the perennial mysteries of married love: How can an act which both people enjoy so much, out of which each person can gain so much personal satisfaction at the sensual, psychological and deepest levels of their being — how can such an act be at the same time one of self-giving love? It should be noted that many married people undoubtedly find considerable satisfaction from the fact that they have contributed to the pleasure of the other. In such cases it may be that the communion of intercourse is a culmination of a real communion in their lives, or communion in which each is actively trying to help the other.

But even deeper than that, it is because their act is a renewal of their marriage covenant that they engage in a simultaneous giving and receiving. As the couple start out upon marriage, it is precisely because they have given of themselves without reservation to the other that they can now receive the beloved. Throughout their married life, it will be precisely because they have each given of themselves, even denied themselves, on behalf of the other that they will reach that state of personal development which is the immediate goal of human life, a state of true inner freedom in regard both to oneself and to other things, a freedom which frees the person for unselfish service towards God and neighbor.

4. Bodily Expression

Another similarity between the Eucharistic and marital communions can be seen in the fact that both are bodily expressions of love. There would be no Eucharist if there had been no Incarnation. In becoming man, the Second Person of the Trinity gave bodily expression to Love. It was a costly expression. We see his weariness, for example, at Jacob's well. Then at the Last Supper he transformed bread and wine into his own body and blood and under this form gave himself to his disciples; the next day this bodily giving was concluded on Calvary. In every Eucharistic communion we re-live this bodily expression of the love of Christ for men.

The marital communion is likewise meant to be a bodily expression of love, and by love we understand here a giving of self. The degree to which a particular marital act of intercourse embodies this giving of self will vary from time to time within the same marriage. The contraceptive question asks whether or not contraceptive intercourse is an authentic embodiment of self-giving. It seems to me that by positively excluding the possibility of future demands, contraception denies a real embodiment of self-giving, that it relegates the "self-giving" to the realm of ideas or intentions.

On the other hand, the parallel with the Eucharistic communion argues that authentically human self-giving cannot be kept intentional but must be fully human, fully incarnate, fully bodily, with all its material and physical consequences so that the Christian may keep the command of the Last Supper: "This is my commandment: love one another, as I have loved you" (Jn 15: 12).

5. Sacrificial Offering

The bodily offering of self that is represented in the Eucharist and in the marriage covenant is also a sacrificial offering. The work of Christ begun in the Last Supper and concluded on Calvary was *the* Sacrifice — not in the sense of just being difficult and painful but in the sense of being *the* offering for the purpose of making men holy. Men can be holy only in God, only as a gift from God, only by being in contact with God. In the Incarnation we have the gift of God to men. Now in the incarnate sacrifice of Christ we have the gift of man to God, the complete self-giving of Christ who opens a new communion between God and man in his sacrificial offering. Union with God is achieved only through sacrifice, the offering of self to God with the hope that the offering is real and will bring down the blessing of holiness.

In marriage, the offering of each to the other without reservation is also a sacrifice. Again, this includes the notion of difficulty but it takes its root meaning from the idea of making holy. It is not that husband can make wife holy or vice versa. Rather it is that both husband and wife will grow in the holiness of Christ according to the measure in which they live up to his call to give of self in order to help build up the other.

St. Paul is explicit in affirming that husbands are to grow in holiness by loving their wives "as Christ loved the Church and sacrificed himself for her" (Eph 5:25). He sacrificed himself that he might sanctify the Church — not as something other than himself but rather as a mystery of extension of himself. Through the sacrifice by the Head, the whole Christ, the Body of Christ, is sanctified, because "the two shall become one." Similarly, the husband who gives of himself for his wife is actually loving himself, for in marriage the spouse only grows in holiness to the extent that he or she grows in giving of self on behalf of the other, a sacrificial offering of self.

6. Sealed through Death

Very closely related to the sacrificial offering is the fact that both the Eucharistic and marital covenants are sealed through a death to self. The New Covenant made by Christ was sealed in his own blood the next day on Calvary. His physical death was the embodiment of his inner death to self. His was an act of complete giving of self, an act of complete obedience, a perfect compliance with the will of the Father without regard to his own inconvenience and suffering. The matrimonial covenant is sealed by sexual intercourse which, if it symbolizes anything, symbolizes a complete mutual giving of self and acceptance of the other. This is brought out in St. Paul's letter to the Ephesians mentioned above. It also relates marriage to the general law of the Christian life: "He who finds his life will lose it; and he who loses his life for my sake will find it" (Mt 10:39).

The purpose in drawing these five comparisons between the Eucharistic and marital communions has been to shed light from the certain on the controversial. In looking at the two communions as sacramental we saw that it would be erroneous to apply the principle of totality to the Eucharistic communion. What is all important is "now," the present state of the believer. He cannot play a percentage morality and state that since most of the time he is open to the sacrifice required by Christian life, he may therefore worthily receive Communion at any time even though he be temporarily alienated from God and unwilling to live the life of love as his present circumstances demand it.

I believe that the same is true of the marital communion. It is insufficient to look at the over-all marriage and its apparent openness to life. As a sacramental action, the marital communion must be judged not in terms of last year or next year but in terms of now.

I think that this same non-contraceptive conclusion has been re-inforced by looking at the Eucharistic and marital communions as renewals of their respective covenants, both of which required faith in the Father, "for better or for worse." By seeing the parallel as a bodily expression of love, a sacrificial offering of self, and as sealed by death to self we can understand the necessity for the bodily action to be a faithful representation of self-giving love, a love which is open to difficulty and founded upon death to self-interest. It seems to me that a very heavy burden of proof lies on the contraceptionist to prove that the act which has positively excluded the risk of the covenant, the risk of having to love more, is really an act of holy communion. I do not think that he can do so, for I believe that contraception separates the symbol of self-giving from the reality.

SECTION III

PRACTICAL CONSIDERATIONS

Chapter Seven

THE PASTORAL PROBLEM

Pope Paul did the entire Church a great favor by the issuance of *Humanae Vitae,* for he forced a growing pastoral problem into the light of day. The subject of contraception was the source of division long before *Humanae Vitae.* It was frequently the unspoken source of suspicion among Catholics. The confusion it was causing was tremendous. This priest said one thing, that one said another, the Pope repeated the tradition. This theologian was for contraception, that one equivocated, and this one sided with the Pope. The bishops, except for a couple of Europeans, generally said nothing.

When I read of the loss of credibility in the Church attributed to the teaching on contraception, I cannot help but ask myself if this is due to its *teaching,* in which case it has been suffering from a lack of credibility for years, or to the lack of uniformity in the pastoral practice. If the Church has become less believable since 1963, the beginning of the public debate in earnest, I cannot help thinking that it has suffered this damage because of the complete confusion existing at the parish level, the pastoral level.

If the Pope had come out with a similar encyclical going along with the practice of contraception, a problem would still exist, although it undoubtedly would be much quieter. It would still be a non-defined teaching, still promulgated unilaterally, and it could still be attacked on the bases of its theology if it followed the majority position paper. The conservatives could take the position that the liberals are now taking; there could still be a divergence of pastoral teachings.

The elements in the pastoral crisis are several. First there is the doctrinal one, the actual teaching about non-contraception. This problem is focused on the quality of the theology in *Humanae Vitae*. Secondly, there is the much wider problem of authority behind this teaching. It has become evident that thousands of modern Catholics no longer believe that the magisterium is given a special guidance by the Holy Spirit in its ordinary teaching (as contrasted with its *ex cathedra* teaching).[1] No longer are they willing to resolve a conflict between their own opinions and the magisterium in favor of the magisterium. It is not a matter of not believing that divine guidance is *limited* to the hierarchy (I know of no one who teaches that) but of believing that, in the case of conflict, the enlightenment of the individual conscience is *superior* to that of the magisterium.

Allied to this is the problem of the bishop who sincerely believes that the Pope has taught rightly and who has priests who teach otherwise. In any business or government organization such a situation would be handled very efficiently. The person would be informed that he was acting directly contrary to corporate or government policy and that he could not continue to do so within that structure. He would either put up and shut up, or he would get out.

Within the Church the problem is considerably more deli-

---

1. It is becoming increasingly apparent that large numbers of Catholics are no longer willing to believe in the teaching authority of the Church as exercised in *ex cathedra* definitions of either Pope or Council. In a recent conversation, a well-educated person who described herself as searching and in touch with the feelings of the people indicated that dogmatic teaching as such was irrelevant. She and people like her simply were not about to accept something as true because it was taught either by the Council of Nicea or Vatican II or by any other formal means of teaching. (This of course runs counter to the explicit theologizing of those theologians who argue for a change in the teaching about contraception, but it certainly has not arisen out of a vacuum.)

cate. On the one hand, the Church teaches the necessity of following one's conscience even if it be erroneous. It proclaims the
worth, the dignity, and the freedom of the individual person.
It knows it cannot force people to accept its teachings. On the
other hand, the bishops have the ultimate local responsibility for
promulgating what the Church teaches to be true. The bishop is
assisted in this by his priests. If a priest refuses to teach an
authoritative pronouncement of the magisterium, the bishop is
faced with a dilemma: his responsibility to do his best to see
that the truth is preached and his inability to force the conscience
of anyone including his priests. If he does nothing, he will give
the impression that he doesn't care or really doesn't believe it
himself; if he suspends the priests, he has a riot of public opinion
to contend with. He is also faced with the embarrassing reality
that in the past he has probably refused to do anything to those
priests who refused to teach the social doctrine of the Church.
It's a very delicate situation indeed.

In addition to the problem of confusion created by outspoken
dissent, there are several other pastoral problems in dealing with
the life of the individual Catholic.

1.   Good Faith and Error

It is axiomatic in moral theology that if you are reasonably
sure that a person who is (1) doing an objective wrong, is (2)
in good faith and (3) would not change if properly informed, you
are not obliged to inform that person of the right way of acting.
In this way, you keep him in good faith and good conscience,
whereas if you tell him that his actions are objectively erroneous,
you may put him in a position where he will continue to act
wrongly but now in bad faith and bad conscience. It seems like
a very logical theory: why put a man in a situation where he will
become guilty of sin? Let him stay ignorant and blameless. Of
course this has to be modified where his actions are causing
grave harm to others.

I must confess that I have always had a hang-up on this

moral theory. No doubt it's very humanistic but it certainly seems to make the biblical Christ either some sort of an ogre out to make people guilty or rather ignorant of the audience to which he spoke. Why did Christ lash out at the hypocrisy of the Scribes and Pharisees? Were they already in bad conscience? Considering their long standing tradition, this would be difficult to assume. Did Christ really think that they would change? Considering his recollection of the fate of the prophets, this is also difficult to assume. Perhaps he spoke for our benefit, not for theirs. If that were so, it would seem that he could have spoken in less impassioned tones. Perhaps he never spoke out against the Scribes and the Pharisees and the biblical passages were only the product of the early Church and the evangelists who wanted to show why he was rejected and criticized. However, even though we may not have the exact words, there still must have been an event in the life of Jesus to give rise to the biblical account. Moreover, why do the *evangelists* want to show the Christ who came to *save* men making some men "guilty" by his preaching?

If these questions can be raised about the condemnations Christ leveled at the actions of some, they can be raised with equal validity about his teaching on sex. His words on the indissolubility of marriage were so shocking that some of the disciples said it would be better never to get married at all (if you couldn't get rid of an unsatisfactory mate). His words on lustful looks and desires have probably brought problems to millions of consciences. Why couldn't Christ have contented himself with the corporal works of mercy and left our consciences to the workings of the Holy Spirit with regard to sex?

I doubt that my qualms about the theological tradition of keeping people in good faith by suppressing the whole message will have any effect on moral theology today. On the other hand, as moral theologians engage in the task of renewing moral theology and basing it firmly on biblical foundations, I can at least wonder about the fate of this tradition. It seems to me that if the gospel is preached and the chips are allowed to fall where they will, we will find that the person whom we feared to put in bad faith may very well not be in bad faith. He may change. Or he may just say that he doesn't believe it or that it doesn't apply to him. The human conscience has a remarkable elasticity, a remarkable ability simply not to admit as personally relevant what the person doesn't think he can achieve right now. Perhaps the "good faith" of those who practice contraception despite the official teaching of the Church will unlock the lips of those who should be promulgating other doctrines including the social, in a more open and evangelistic way.

However, given the traditional reticence to risk putting a person in bad faith, we will continue to have a plurality of pastoral practice and the continuation of confusion. The couple who are told by their favorite priest that there is nothing wrong in their practice of contraception could be hearing this from a priest who either opposed *Humanae Vitae* or who believed it but figured that this couple in front of him did not accept it and would not follow its norm no matter what he said. In this latter case he might say, "Just follow your conscience," or "There's nothing wrong here for you," in an effort to keep the couple in the Church and in good faith. If this priest were very socially minded, it would be interesting to hear his counsel to this same couple if they were organizing a movement to keep Negroes from moving into their apartment building; or on the contrary if they were planning an inter-racial wife-swapping weekend in order to develop real community. Would he content himself with, "Follow your conscience?" I mention this only to show that traditional moral theology has the means of continuing a plurality of teaching and practice on the pastoral level no matter how strongly the Pope and bishops may teach at the doctrinal level. Aside from a change in the theory of good faith, I see no way in which we will or can avoid a plurality of pastoral advice, practice, and confusion.

Out of the inevitable plurality, several things will happen. Catholics will come to realize that advice or guidance given to one couple is not meant to be taken as guidance for all. The advice could very well be a sincere effort to keep someone from leaving the Church altogether; it may amount to an effort to keep the person in good faith even though it means the continuation of an erroneous conscience.

Catholics will also come to consider very lightly the opinion of any single priest or theologian or even groups of them. More and more the teacher will have to show the bases of his teaching, whether it be firmly anchored in Scripture or solidly rooted in tradition; whether it be his personal interpretation or that of the magisterium, etc.; whether it be based on the authority of the Church teaching or solely on reason. Those who claim reason to be the basis for their teaching are going to have to be prepared to demonstrate it. The authority of the individual priest-teacher will be greatly diminished. Those who continue to believe at all will do so out of an increased faith in the Church, even though such faith is now under severe attack. As we come out of the present phase, however, the would-be believer, confronted by a plethora of theologies and conflicting doctrines in the Catholic Church, will once again ask which of all the voices has a claim to be the voice of God, the guarantee of the Apostolic teachings. My guess is that out of the present confusion and the conflict of voices, those who are interested in believing what is true will respond to the teachings of the Church regarding infallibility and ordinary moral certainty. I believe they will do this out of more or less traditional norms of credibility. Others will have different criteria. Some may look to the Church boasting the most generous per capita members; they may become Mormons. Some may look to the Church with the most enthusiastic liturgies; they may become Pentecostals. Some may look for greater involvement in humanitarian causes; they may become Unitarians; etc. But there will be many who will have seen the *sensus fidelium* of the people under Moses, at the time of the Prophets, in New Testament Corinth, during times of slavery, at times of selective wealth and poverty and who will conclude that the feelings of the masses are not a very sure guide in moral matters. They will look elsewhere and a renewed apologetics will make sense to them even if it brings difficulty.

2. The Call to Perfection

Running contrary to the tradition of not disturbing a person in erroneous good faith is the renewed emphasis on the call to perfection for all Christians. This is at the heart of the renewal of moral theology. The call to perfection, once seen as an ideal to be pursued only by the professionally religious is now seen as addressed to all who accept Christ. The laity are thus no longer regarded as capable of becoming only mediocre Christians, second class citizens in God's Church. Rather, they are seen as having co-responsibility for the mission of the Church; they are also co-responsible with the hierarchy and the religious in answering the call of Christ to perfection; they are co-responsible for the Church's authentic expression of her faith consciousness.

Obviously the manner in which they exercise this responsibility and the call to perfection will differ among laymen and between laity and the professionally identified members of the Church — priests, bishops, and religious.

Relevant to the debate of *non-contraception* versus *contraception* is the question of whether the stated teaching of the Church or the practice of contraception better accommodates the call to perfection. I have already indicated why I think the refusal to practice contraception contributes to the development of a number of Christian virtues in a way that does not seem possible with the practice of contraception. More to the point, however, is the fundamental question that married couples must ask themselves: If Christ were a married man living in our circumstances, would he practice contraception? Pope Paul has answered "No," and the vast majority of the national hierarchies of the world have seconded the papal teaching. Some have also emphasized the good faith of the erroneous conscience and the non-culpability of some couples in some circumstances.

The bishops and their assisting priests to whom falls the huge responsibility of leading their people to perfection have a real pastoral problem. They first of all have to believe that the laity are capable of answering Christ's call to perfection. The history of the promulgation of the social doctrine of the Church suggests that many of the clergy either do not believe in it or that they do not believe that the masses of the laity are ready to hear and accept it. If the promulgation of the sexual doctrine of the Church is given the same kind of treatment as the social doctrine has been given for the past seventy-five years, we can expect a very prosperous and comfortable European and North American Church.

The answer is surely not an all-out acceptance of the social doctrine of the Church and an all-out repudiation of her sexual doctrine or vice versa. The call to perfection which our religious leaders must sound loud and clear (and to which they must teach us to respond by their own example as well as by word) must be based solidly on the life and teaching of Christ. In the life and doctrine of Jesus we find *both* the preaching and the living of a social doctrine which hardly condoned the personal amassing of wealth *and* a sexual doctrine that was elevated, difficult to hear, and unacceptable to many of his contemporaries.

Jesus ran no popularity contest. Nor did the prophets before him. Nor did the apostles after him. Bishops and priests who try to play the popularity game by telling people what they want to hear so that the important work of the Church (i.e., fund drives, debt payment) may go on without interruption may find that they have missed a great opportunity to lead their people in answering the call of Christ to perfection. The never ending pastoral problem is the challenge of inspiring a people who are surrounded by a philosophy of pragmatic materialism to realize the values and the teaching of Christ in their own lives.

3.   Helping Those Who Need It   (*See also Appendix I*).

An unseen and silent pastoral problem concerns help to those who need it. Despite all that can be said for natural sterility during the complete nursing period [2] and for the relative efficiency of

_____

2. Sheila K. Kippley, *Breastfeeding and Natural Child Spacing: The Ecology of Natural Mothering* (Baltimore: Penguin, 1975). (Cloth library edition by Harper and Row, 1974.)

natural birth control through periodic continence,[3] some families are going to feel the burden of larger families. In the past, the attitude has been pretty much one of rugged individualism. The larger family had to go it alone. It was their own "fault" for having several children. There was no help coming from the parish community.

The problem of the larger family has been duplicated thousands of times by the family in some other sort of need. In some parishes, a parish organization helps to take care of the very needy, but in others there is nothing. When I first wrote this, I was living in a parish in Canada, a parish that had about $120,000 in the bank and an annual income-to-expense ratio of about 2:1. It was a prosperous, middle class parish, but every once in a while somebody had an extremely difficult time. I had spoken with people who were alienated from the Church because when they asked for some help, there was none forthcoming. I mentioned to a few parishioners that I felt that the parish should be able to help a family that was really down on its luck. Some agreed with me, but one who had the pastor's ear was horrified. "John, we'd have all the poor people in town moving into our parish if we did that!" The next thing I knew I was being accused of being somewhat socialistic in my teachings of Christian doctrine. Needless to say, such a policy would be the very opposite of socialism. I advocated helping our own at the local level; socialism puts all redistribution of resources in the hands of the State.

For years now we have read that the "Church" should sponsor projects to help families who want to use the rhythm process. Perhaps those who control the finances of the Church have done so; however, I am aware of little such sponsorship. If it has been undertaken, the public relations process has been very silent.

At the same time, we are in a period when the relevancy of the geographic parish is being seriously questioned. Is the geographic parish a community? Can it become a community? How can it become more of a community?

---

3. 1976. The possibility of large families due to surprise pregnancies is much less than imagined when this was first written in 1970.

It seems to me that the challenges of the needs of others present a natural unifying force toward community. Why could not the parish community assist some families at the time of childbirth? Why cannot the parish community help the parents of a child who needs an operation not covered by insurance? Why cannot a family in a temporary streak of bad times be helped, if it wants help, by the parish community?

Certainly there would be a few freeloaders. Certainly there would have to be certain qualifications; certainly there would have to be a generous spirit of giving on the part of all parishioners and a real sense of Christian mission on the part of the administrators. All of these things, however, could be worked out if there was a community desire to be mutually helpful in this way. Moreover, for the couple who are expecting a child, it would form a special sense of community support if they knew that unexpected complications and expenses not covered by insurance were not going to drive them into a huge debt.

Humanae Vitae has offered all sorts of challenges — challenges to the individual couple, challenges to theologians, challenges to our faith. I think it has also raised a challenge to the parish community to help those people who will need help as a result of being faithful to the teaching of the Church. It raises a challenge to the administrators of Church funds to do something about sponsoring various kinds of research. It should not be hoping for too much to trust that in a period of intended renewal in the Church many of these challenges will be met.

4.   Breastfeeding and Natural Child Spacing

Since I have perhaps made a contribution towards the continuation of what is a burden to many, I also feel somewhat obliged to do all that I can to lighten that load.

It is not uncommon in the popular discussion of birth control to hear arguments that run something like this: (1) People shouldn't starve. (2) But people are starving in an overpopulated India. (3) Therefore, we should practice contraception. The logician can show the fallacy of the argument on logical grounds, but no one should deny that it expresses the gut reaction of many. The problems of India (which has about every problem in the book, population density being only one of them) raise a sympathetic chord. However, the reaction is generally not a donation to India but a concentration on the population problem of one's own family. The interests of most people are centered close to home, and the problems of the individual family size are felt more keenly than the gigantic problems of India.

Sometimes it is not just the size of the family that is the problem but the frequency. No one who has ever raised children will remain unsympathetic to the mother whose children are born at intervals of only a year. The humorists refer to children born less than one year apart as "Catholic twins," but there is little enough humor in caring for essentially two babies — one who has just passed his first birthday and the newborn infant. As a father whose virtue of patience is in continual need of further development, I share with many other parents the desire for a breathing spell between babies, a desire to get one well-started before a younger brother or sister comes along.

I am also convinced that the Creator has arranged for a natural spacing of children through breastfeeding. I have mentioned this in theology classes for adults and have met many a hurried objection. In every class there was somebody who knew somebody else who nursed her baby and became pregnant while doing so. I am willing to wager that practically everyone of these "nursing mothers" who became pregnant was in fact a "weaning mother," that is, one who was no longer supplying 100% of the baby's food and drink but had started the baby on other foods.

Thus when I speak of natural spacing through breastfeeding, I am referring essentially to 100% natural breastfeeding. Mothers who are providing for the complete nutritional needs of their children through breastfeeding are almost guaranteed of not becoming pregnant during this period. How long can this period last? Among mothers who take breastfeeding seriously, it is by no means uncommon for them to continue the 100% process for six, eight or nine months. Then as the baby's appetite increases, the gradual weaning process begins. For some time, perhaps another three to six months, the baby will continue to derive as much quantitative nourishment from its mother as before, and the needs of its increased appetite are taken care of by other foods. Some mothers continue the nursing-weaning process up to two years; others wean the baby earlier. Many find that the baby just weans itself somewhere between age one and two with no coaxing or holding back by the mother.

Is this hopeful daydreaming or is it real? I am fortunate in being married to a woman who is interested in breastfeeding both for personal reasons and for what might be called professional reasons. Her personal experience and her talks with other mothers led her to write a manual on breastfeeding and the side effects of child-spacing.[4] The research she uncovered points overwhelmingly to the fact that 100% breastfeeding with the absence of any menstrual periods is about 99% effective in postponing pregnancy. Menstruation and ovulation may be delayed until 12 or even 18 months after childbirth through proper breastfeeding and gradual weaning at a later date.

If this is so, why don't mothers know about it? Why hasn't the Church promoted it? First of all, regarding the Church, despite much lip service paid by official documents to the necessity of research in the area of family planning, I have seen precious few announcements of hierarchical sponsorship of such research. Perhaps a few dollars have been allocated here and there, but by and large there has been an all too typical attitude of "wait and see." Official hopes seems to have been centered almost exclusively on the development of a new pill which will regulate, not suppress, the monthly ovulatory cycle. I certainly hope that such a drug can be formulated, but it is certainly näive to expect the big pharmaceutical houses to spend dollars to research a natural, non-drug-using means of child spacing such as breastfeeding. I feel that generally speaking the teachers in the Church have been negligent in this

---

4. Sheila K. Kippley, *op. cit.*

area. The burden has been re-affirmed but little or no help has been given to lighten that burden.

Secondly, perhaps the reason why most mothers are unaware of this natural means of child-spacing and why Church teachers seem similarly unaware is that all too many doctors are unaware. This may seem an unfair indictment of the medical profession, but it is true. Many of them learn almost nothing about the natural process of breastfeeding in medical school; their education centers around disease, and any problems of the nursing mother are situated in terms of various formulas. In our family we have had personal experience to substantiate this, and my wife's friends have experienced this also. Some doctors simply will not believe the child-spacing effect of proper 100% nursing regardless of how many studies substantiate it.

Other doctors refuse to believe that a baby can be healthy when nourished only on its mother's milk. Again, we have had the experience of mothers supplying 100% of the baby's nourishment and having a moral crisis with the doctor. The doctor tells them how healthy the baby is and then asks what foods the baby is taking. The mother replies that she is breastfeeding. The doctor says she'll have to stop that and tells her what foods to start. The mother just disregards the advice as ill-founded. At the next periodic checkup, the doctor once again exclaims, "What a healthy and happy baby you have." Then he starts the food routine. The mother, especially if she is a young mother, now is in a dilemma. Should she be honest and admit that she has disregarded his advice or should she lie and keep him happy? It is not easy for many young women to tell their doctors they have not followed his advice, especially when the doctor has just put himself in the position of admitting it was superfluous by his comments on the fine health of the baby. I recommend the direct, painfully honest approach as being the only one which will educate certain sections of our medical profession about the nutritional advantages of breastfeeding exclusive of pablum, bottles, etc. When both doctors and mothers come to realize that breastfeeding is an excellent and nutritious form of feeding a baby, then the first year of the baby's life will be healthier and happier for both baby and mother.[5]

This is by no means a wholesale indictment of the medical profession. Anyone investigating the relationship between the profession and breastfeeding mothers will quickly realize that the strongest source of criticism of some doctors is the doctor who has more academic and personal experience with breastfeeding mothers and their babies. My problem with many doctors is that they are discouraging a process which is humanly beautiful, healthy for the baby both nutritionally and emotionally, satisfying for the mother, and which has the side effect of spacing children. (As a husband, I can point to the additional advantage of never having to warm up a bottle.)

Nothing I can say in the few last pages will suffice to dispel the general skepticism in this regard, nor can I describe the process of breastfeeding which we believe is the fully natural process. The best I can do at this point is to recommend to interested mothers, skeptics, and other interested parties that they review the research that has been made in this field and form their own conclusions. The books recommended in this section were both written to provide this kind of information especially for those mothers who want to nurse their babies but have unfortunately been told that it was a good way to get pregnant again.

---

5. Perhaps the greatest source of help to the nursing mother in our time has been the La Leche League International, 9616 Minneapolis Ave., Franklin Park, Illinois, 60131. It started in 1956 with a handful of mothers concerned with breastfeeding and has since spread all over North America. Their handbook, *The Womanly Art of Breastfeeding*, has been a help to thousands of mothers who desire to nurse their babies.

APPENDIX I

MODERN NATURAL FAMILY PLANNING

1. Terminology. The term "rhythm" as used in the text of this book, first written in 1970, refers to any and all methods of birth regulation based upon knowledge of a woman's periodic fertility and infertility. However, in common usage, "rhythm" refers to "calendar rhythm," the system devised by Doctors Ogino and Knaus in 1930 and based solely on *past* records of cycle length. While for a general population it provided an effectiveness roughly in the same ball park with the barrier methods (condom, diaphragm), it proved to be quite unreliable for women whose menstrual cycles were fairly irregular. Furthermore, too much calendar rhythm was not based on the Ogino-Knaus calculations but instead relied on hearsay and guesswork. The combination of inherent defects plus misapplication resulted in a bad reputation for the term rhythm. Thus, current usage (1976) tends to use the term rhythm to mean "calendar rhythm" and uses "natural family planning" to designate modern systems of fertility awareness that are based on current observations of the symptoms of fertility.

2. Contemporary systems. The most complete system is called the full sympto-thermal method. It uses primarily the regular observations of changes that occur in a) the cervix, b) cervical mucus, and c) basal temperature levels in such a way that the various symptoms provide a corroboration or

crosscheck on each other. Other systems use only the mucus symptom or only the temperature sign.

3. Effectiveness. A standard way of expressing effectiveness rates is "so many pregnancies per 100 woman years of use-exposure." On that basis, the sympto-thermal system has shown an effectiveness of less than 1 surprise pregnancy per 100 woman years. This is a very high effectiveness rate that equals or surpasses rates for the Pill and IUD, and one that can be attained by well instructed and motivated couples.[1]

4. Providing help. An organization that is trying to provide NFP assistance is the Couple to Couple League (CCL) which was founded in 1971 by the author and his wife and aided greatly by Konald Prem, M.D., Professor of Obstetrics and Gynecology at the University of Minnesota School of Medicine. A goal of CCL is to provide adequate instruction about natural family planning in every community throughout the country. Its written teaching tool is a 238 page manual, *The Art of Natural Family Planning,* and it likewise publishes an informative membership newsletter five times a year. Further information about the League and its services may be obtained by writing the Couple to Couple League, P.O. Box 11084, Cincinnati, Ohio 45211.

---

1. Josef Roetzer. *Archiv* for Gynakologie, (206) 1968, pp. 195-214.

APPENDIX II

CONTINUED DISSENT:

IS IT RESPONSIBLE LOYALTY?

Reprinted by permission from *Theological Studies*, (March, 1971), 428 E. Preston Street, Baltimore, Md. 21202.

Three recent magazine items have intrigued me with the possibility of their relationships. One was the series of articles in *America* devoted to the issue of loyalty and dissent;[1] the other was John Milhaven's *Critic* article "A New Sense of Sin";[2] the third was the *Look* article on the Presbyterian debate about sex.[3] The *America* series generally propounded the viewpoint that the dissent that has centered around *Humanae Vitae* has been an exercise of responsible loyalty to the Church despite any appearances to the contrary. The Milhaven article noted that the theologians who opened the doors to contraception did so by discarding an approach to natural law and in doing so had also discarded the rationale for the traditional Catholic doctrine prohibiting all extramarital sexual behavior. This, I take it, would include masturbation, premarital and extramarital sex, homosexuality, and nongenital intercourse. The question thus raised is obvious: If the dissent from *Humanae Vitae*

1. *America*, June 27, 1970.
2. John Milhaven, "A New Sense of Sin," *Critic*, March-April, 1970, pp. 14-21.
3. Jack Star, "The Presbyterian Debate Over Sex," *Look*, Aug. 11, 1970, pp. 54-60.

likewise *logically* includes dissent from the entire Christian sexual doctrine, is such dissent in fact responsible, is it an example of theological loyalty to the Church?

Certainly there must be those who would welcome the repudiation of the entire Catholic tradition about sex. Talk about guidelines, personal values and decisions, exceptions to the general norm, the over-all trend, freedom and responsibility is ever so much more palatable than talk about universal norms and negatives, faithful obedience to the law of Christ, and an objective standard of what it means to become fully human. The situation ethics which has been enshrined in the main section of the Presbyterian report certainly must have its supporters among Catholics. However, the question is not whether certain Catholics would welcome a new sex ethic that is devoid of absolutes and would rejoice in the day that the original Presbyterian proposal (as it came from the theologians and before it was amended by some "conservatives" who wanted to keep calling some things sinful) became generally and openly accepted by the Catholic Church. The questions raised by the dissent are rather (1) whether the premises on which the dissent is based can avoid becoming a *de facto* situation ethic; (2) whether such an ethic can avoid a logical outcome such as the original Presbyterian proposal; (3) whether such an ethic is loyal to Christ. If such an ethic is not loyal to Christ and if it is the logical outcome of the sexual theology of dissent, then the doctrinal dissent from *Humanae Vitae* must be seen to be neither loyal nor responsible. The dissent can also be seen as something less than responsible if it has treated the whole matter as a purely rational, philosophical argument and if it has used the adversary ethic of the courtroom lawyer in such a way as to create some one-sided impressions.

In my treatment of these questions, certain limitations should be noted. First, my observations are limited. With one exception, they are limited to the American scene, and even then they are few in number. However, it is my conviction that this limited sampling is indicative of the dissent in America. I admit that I am not well enough acquainted with the European dissent to judge its similarity to or difference from that in North America.

Secondly, the limited selection tends to make the argumentation somewhat *ad hominem.* I make no apologies for this: it is just the fact that a few theologians have written rather frequently on dissent and sexual morality, and I believe that they have a significant influence in American Catholic theologizing as it takes place in universities and colleges, seminaries, parish adult education, and even in the secondary and elementary Catholic schools and CCD classes. The significant point, as I see it, is that these theologians are somewhat corporate personalities, summing up a pervasive theological perspective. It is in this sense that I think it is valid to use their statements as representative of the position of dissent and of trends in the theology of sex in North America.

Thirdly, the concern of this article is with current approaches in moral theology. This makes it an article on methodology. At the same time it will be apparent that my interest in methodology derives from a primary interest in Christian sexuality. Different approaches and different presuppositions lead to different conclusions, and the growing public departure from the biblical norms of sexuality has not occurred without the adoption of some new approaches.

The article is written from the viewpoint of a realist interpretation of Scripture. That is, I accept as true that God has somehow revealed what is good for man in Scripture. Thus, the condemnations of adultery, fornication, etc., are not simply the human understanding of Jesus and Paul or a projection of their own celibacy, nor are they simply a reflection of the times. I accept, through my understanding of the living tradition of the Church, the interpretation that in this area of human behavior we have in Scripture a concrete norm for men of all time and not just a reflection valid for the men of bygone days.

Traditionally, Catholic moralists have said that such norms are of the natural law or the order of creation; then they have proceeded to show the inherent human reasonableness of such norms — since it surely seemed reasonable to assume that we should be able to demonstrate the rationality of whatever is believed to be natural to man. Much of this reasoning was in terms of the effects, and as long as the effects remained the same and were still thought evil, the evil of the original action was seen. For example, fornication was explained as evil because of the risk of a child being born without a regular family structure. Reduced risks today then lead to fewer "evil" effects and the evil of fornication becomes questioned. When the evil of an action (e.g., fornication) is not so clearly seen today in terms of the older explanation, the question is raised about the relationship between a Christian moral teaching and the evidence or argumentation we can mount for it. Does a Christian moral teaching held forth as being of the order of creation derive its primary force from the teaching authority of the Church and its Scripture or from the clarity of the evidence and argumentation? How much of a "clarity gap" can there be? It is my opinion that the practical force of a moral doctrine for the man of faith derives from the teaching authority of the Church and its Scripture, although the ultimate force comes from its being grounded in the order of creation. Furthermore, at times we shall be quite wanting for "proofs" in morality in a manner not dissimilar to our efforts to "prove" something else that the biblical authors take for granted: that the observer of creation should be able to discern it as the handiwork of the Creator.

Furthermore, I think that the apparent difficulties in establishing the reasonableness of a moral doctrine will be closely related to the proximity that the particular practice has to the "will to freedom." Modern atheism, as typified by Sartre, is a premise, a will to freedom; so perhaps is much of current sexuality. In each case the historical argument may be the most effective in the long run. What happens to a people when atheism becomes the order of the day? Perhaps regimes such as Nazism and Communism have already told us, and novels such as George Orwell's *1984* and Aleksandr Solzhenitzyn's *The First Circle* continue to dramatize it. What happens to a people when free love becomes the accepted mode? Does Aldous Huxley show us in *Brave New World?*

A Christian is free to believe that, in an effort to spare man the consequences of having to find out empirically about the effects of atheism and hedonism, God in His revelation has been rather explicit about both belief and sexuality. If we can say that it is natural, of the very order of creation, for man to recognize his Creator and not flinch from admitting the gap between our reasons and the act of faith, we should not be ashamed to admit a gap between our reasons for the Christian sexual ethic and our faith in it. In the last analysis, the traditional sex ethic says that sexual actions have a certain transcendental significance about them, and the methodology of empiricism simply cannot transcend the physical to arrive at such a spiritual valuation. As we progress farther into a civilization which denies its Judeo-Christian foundation, we can expect an increasing divergence between the moral vision of those who have consciously or unconsciously adopted contemporary secular premises and those who retain the Christian tradition. It is not a question of facts, as it was with Galileo; the new revolution is a question of values.

I am quite sure that much more needs to be said about the relationship of the religious ethic and the clarity of evidence we can produce for it, but the foregoing remarks should serve at least to delineate the position from which this article is written. Others may be convinced that the apparent clarity gap needs to be bridged by accepting what seems reasonable to people of today and changing the traditional Christian ethic accordingly. My criticism of the current dissent stems at least partly from a conviction that a methodology that seeks to build a Christian ethic on what is clear and reasonable to contemporary man is building on sand. A second reason for my criticism of the dissent is that, as seen in the light of the earlier model in Protestantism, the process of dissent historically begins with the area of less clarity, contraception, and moves steadily forward into the topics of premarital and extramarital sex, areas certainly noted for a greater biblical clarity. Whether or not theologians and contemporary man will find greater clarity of evidence to support the Christian tradition in these areas is something to be considered, because it is not impossible that someday we may have the Catholic equivalent of the Presbyterian report. These general concerns are spelled out in what follows.

I

To start with the mode of presentation first, has the theology of dissent used the representational ethic of the courtroom lawyer and the collective bargaining agent as contrasted with the communitarian ethic of the professional arbitrator in its argumentation? That is, has it tended to leave a one-sided and perhaps misleading impression?

First, the special qualification of *Humanae Vitae* as a non-infallible teaching can be misleading (regardless of the source of the label). For all that any of us know, it may in fact be infallible in the same way that the teaching about the divinity of Christ was infallible prior to Nicaea and prior to the development of the dogmatic note of infallibility. That is, if a teaching is true, it is so regardless of the dogmatic note attached to it. Secondly, and more to the point, the singling out of *Humanae Vitae* for this treatment carries with it a possibly misleading impression when no such mention of noninfallibility is regularly attached to other statements of popes and bishops. For example, it is difficult for me to imagine a theologian writing on the social order and qualifying his references to *Pacem in terris* and *Populorum progressio* with repeated statements that in these documents the pontiffs were teaching noninfallibly and that the faithful should give them respectful attention but should not feel bound by them in forming their consciences. Certainly, if pressed, he would admit the nondefined character of such teachings, as he would have to admit the nondefined status of teaching about the dignity of man, infanticide, and any other moral teaching. Furthermore, it is difficult to imagine anyone saying that because such documents as the social encyclicals failed to carry the dogmatic note of infallibility, the burden of proof remained on the magisterium. The point I am trying to make is that the *regular* treatment of *Humanae Vitae* by dissenting theologians in this *singular* way leaves a one-sided impression. Furthermore, if every reference to the ordinary magisterium as exercised in social encyclicals and Vatican II were couched in the language of reservation, what would be the effect?

A related question concerns whether the subject of authority has been given anything like equal treatment regarding the Pope and the papal birth-control commission (hereafter PBCC). Has it been made clear to the Catholic people who have listened to the dissent that the PBCC possessed no theological authority? Or, in fact, has not the impression been made that contraception is approved by the Holy Spirit, who made His will known through the authority of the majority position? My affirmative response to the last question leads directly to the second point at issue: whether the dissent has treated an essentially religious matter as a purely philosophical one.

II

The criticism of *Humanae Vitae* has fallen into three categories: (1) it was not a collegial statement; (2) it was not promulgated as infallible; (3) its philosophy did not convince the dissenters. My question about responsible dissent asks whether the philosophy of the majority position of the PBCC report has convinced the majority of dissenters. The core argument of that document treated the individual marital sex act as deriving its morality from the totality of sex acts in the marriage. In my opinion, the argument is quickly reduced to something like absurdity simply by treating extramarital sex acts in the same way. Does the mutually out-in-the-open, key-club-weekend extramarital sex take its morality from the over-all general fidelity of the partners, or is such behavior to be branded as adultery regardless of intention? I could not claim to have read all the literature on dissent, but in what I have read I have found not a single argument based on the cogency of the philosophy of the PBCC; and I think this is

due to the poverty of the position. The references to the fact
that the PBCC *majority* stated a judgment are simply appeals
to authority. It seems to me that fairness, loyalty, and responsible dissent would include a criticism of the PBCC majority
philosophy, when similar criticisms are made about *Humanae
Vitae*.[4]

Furthermore, I have seen nothing in the theology of dissent
which points out that it is impossible to provide arguments
about moral behavior that are convincing to all in a society of
pluralistic practices, even to all men of good will. Here I think
Paul VI may be open to criticism for his apparent naivete in
thinking that "men of our day are particularly capable of seizing
the deeply reasonable and human character of this fundamental principle," i.e., the inseparable connection of the unitive
and procreative aspects of the conjugal sex act. However, if
Paul VI is to be criticized for wishful thinking here, it should
also be mentioned that even the PBCC majority position saw
the union of the unitive and procreative aspects as the fulness
to which the contraceptive acts were ordered and from which
they received their morality. It is easy to understand how
Paul VI, seeing the reasoning of those who advocated contraception, might have thought that the norm of inseparability
was apparent in general to men of our day. It is becoming
increasingly evident that in no area of sexual morality is there
universal rational agreement. Nor is there such agreement
among Christians even on matters of life and death; one only
has to observe the statements on abortion issued by the Lutheran
Church of America and other Protestant bodies, and this in
the face of the strongest statements by such Protestant theologians as Dietrich Bonhoeffer, Karl Barth, and Helmut Thielicke
to the effect that abortion is murder pure and simple.

Give the fact that Christian morality never has been nor
ever will be identical with philosophical ethics, is it really

---

4. Such a criticism is provided in at least one article of dissent: M. John
Farrelly, O.S.B., "The Principle of the Family Good," *Theological
Studies* 31 (1970) 262-74.

responsible and loyal to the Church to dismiss out of hand a reaffirmation of one of the most ancient moral traditions in Christianity on the basis that it is not philosophically agreeable today? The immediate objection is that a matter of natural law should be demonstrable to all men, not just believing, submissive Roman Catholics. I have tried to anticipate this by showing that even in what I consider a much more obvious area of natural law such as abortion, such demonstration simply is not working today. The truth of the matter is that in the area of human behavior we can arrive at moral certitude, but the person who wants to disagree will always find room for dissent. Since other areas of morality are not proposed to rest purely on philosophical ethics, it seems less than responsible to disregard the tradition affirmed by *Humanae Vitae* on the grounds that its rationale is not totally convincing philosophically — unless at the same time the dissent questions and disregards every other area of morality in which the philosophy fails to convince all.

There are, most likely, some who will agree that this is precisely the job of moral theology today: to criticize every traditionally accepted moral norm and to conclude that those which cannot be supported in a rational way that is convincing to all should be dropped as archaic accretions. This process is fairly well under way in situation ethics; as far as sex is concerned, the results are pretty well in. It is, for all practical purposes, impossible to prove that any given sexual act is always wrong. For example, the older reasons against adultery showing the dangers of broken homes simply fall by the wayside before a people who accept or at least tolerate adultery. Such sociological reasons are meaningless before people who mutually agree to participate in weekend key clubs. It seems to me that the most a modern philosophical ethic can do is to conclude with situation ethics that we should be loving, loyal, and helpful according to the demands of the situation. If a couple after thoughtful consideration decided it was loving etc. to join a weekend key club, the ultimate rational judgment would center around their responsible personal considerations, not the act called material adultery by the older ethic. A philosophic ethic stops at what seems reasonable to men, but the reasonableness of men may be foolishness in the sight of God.

A religious ethic, on the other hand, does not claim to be solely rational, i.e., to be dependent solely upon its ability to demonstrate the reasonableness of its claims to the men of its times. It relies for its real force on the loyalty of men to their religious covenant. It is, if you will, a loyalty ethic rather than a philosophical ethic. The Christian religious ethic does not, or at least should not, presume to be able to prove to all why adultery is wrong either in general or in every case. It simply affirms that God, who knows what is best for full human development, has forbidden the practice of adultery. The theologian is free, and perhaps even obliged, to explain the evil of adultery in the terms of his day, but he will never fully succeed, for the simple reason that he can never adequately and fully understand what it means to be human, much less what it means to be an adopted son of God.

Regarding contraception, the Christian ethic will scarcely be able to do a better job of explaining its evil than it can with regard to the more evident question of adultery. It is once again a question of a loyalty ethic based on the belief that God calls the married couple to be open to the risk of transmitting life.

The basis for this belief at the present time is a general belief that the Church has been guided by the Spirit in its basic doctrine of marital noncontraception. As the Episcopalian priest Robert Farrar Capon noted in *Bed and Board*, it is a little difficult to believe that the Christian Church, which until 1930 taught unanimously against contraception, has suddenly been shown to be in error.[5] I would add that the difficulty is compounded when we are asked to believe that the tradition has been shown to be in error by modern man who is likewise

---

5. Robert Farrar Capon, *Bed and Board: Plain Talk About Marriage* (New York, 1965) p. 87.

showing us attitudes and practices of sex such that we can
only ask "Can you call it anything above degradation?"

This belief, grounded on the ordinary magisterium, as is
Catholic belief about adultery, may likewise be shown to be
at least somewhat grounded in Scripture. The criticism that
has fallen on the "sin of Onan" has not yet provided adequate
reason to show why only Onan merited death for his transgres-
sion of the levirate when his father and younger brother were
likewise guilty of breaking the levirate in the same circumstances.[6] Nor has the levirate theory shown why Onan received
death when the Jewish punishment as recorded in Scripture
was simply an insult to the offender by the aggrieved woman
in the presence of the elders.[7] I have submitted in *Covenant,
Christ and Contraception* that an adequate explanation has to
take into account the manner in which Onan violated the
levirate covenant, his going through the motions which he then
invalidated by contraception.[8]

In a manner similar to the defense of the Catholic doctrine
about adultery, a theology based on the biblical notion of
covenant may be employed in an effort to provide a reasonable
explanation. However, all such explanations are doomed to
fall short of being fully adequate, for the simple reasons adduced
before: our limitations in understanding ourselves as personal
creatures, self-determining and yet called to be obedient as
adopted sons of God.

Of course, this raises a question: "Do we have here a tradition embodying the work of the Spirit or merely a human
tradition which is simply old?" I cannot see how this can be
answered on a purely rational basis, since the working of the
Spirit is not a subject of demonstration. Thus the dilemma: if
the subject matter itself cannot be conclusively proved on the
basis of philosophical ethics (a problem common to all areas

---

6. Gn 38:6-26. In v. 26 Judah admits his guilt: "This comes of my
not giving her to my son Shelah, to be his wife."
7. Dt 25:5-10.
8. John F. Kippley, *Covenant, Christ and Contraception* (Staten Island,
N.Y., 1970) pp. 17-19.

of morality) and if we cannot prove conclusively in religious ethics that the tradition is of the Spirit (a problem likewise common to all areas of morality, in that no area of human behavior has been defined *de fide*), then are we not left with a practical moral agnosticism?

It seems to me that one can resolve this question either by following the path of situation ethics and the language of radical personalism or by following the path of the religious covenant. The former admits that the historical tradition provides certain insights and guidelines but stresses that in the last analysis the person, in order to become more fully person, must make his own code and his own decisions about what is right and wrong for him to do here and now.

The morality of the religious covenant reminds the believer that God has not revealed Himself through logical demonstration, that the scandal of Christianity, according to Bultmann, is the call to faith in Jesus, the call to be obedient to Him.[9] It says that the road to becoming more fully a person is the acceptance of Christ as Word and norm, and involves death to self. It admits that certain material norms associated with interpersonal relations are universally binding. It holds that the great moral tradition of the covenanted Church is binding on all and that the burden of proof is upon those who would change it.

This brings us to a crucial point in the examination of whether the dissent from *Humanae Vitae* has been responsible or not. On whom is the burden of proof? If the burden rests upon the tradition, it seems that we are faced with the moral agnosticism mentioned previously; for I cannot see, aside from the covenant of faith and loyalty, how anyone can prove that a given interpersonal action is always wrong. The most (it seems to me at this time) that the tradition can demonstrate is that its sexual doctrine is internally consistent and in full accord with Scripture and covenant theology. This I think I

9. Rudolph Bultmann, *Jesus Christ and Mythology* (New York, 1958) chap. 3.

have done in *Covenant, Christ and Contraception*.[10] It can further show that contradictory approaches lead to what is moral chaos in terms of the religious covenant. To assert that the burden of proof rests continually on the tradition seems tantamount to treating the entire matter exclusively as a subject of philosophical ethics.

If it is true, as Richard McCormick has suggested, that the only thing actually guaranteed by an ancient moral tradition is its age, it nevertheless is given a weight of probability not to be lightly dismissed in terms of the religious covenant. The burden of proof falls upon those who would seek to show that the presumed guidance of the Spirit in the moral tradition was really only the prudence of men. If it be accepted, then, that the burden is upon the advocates of contraception, what is the evidence for change?[11]

III

We are back to the key question of this essay, which asks in a critical tone whether the dissent from *Humanae Vitae* has been an exercise in responsible loyalty to the Church. Does the rationale behind the dissent result in a *de facto* situation ethic, and if so, is it loyal to Christ and His Church?

It might be well to look briefly at some of the premises of dissent; I think it fair to say that Charles E. Curran represents this point of view in an articulate way and thus provides a fair point of reference. Fr. Curran mentions three contemporary philosophical approaches, all of which "would deny the absolute conclusion of the papal encyclical in condemning all means of artificial birth control."[12] The transcendental method

---

10. *Op. cit.*, chap. 5, "Toward a Unified Theory of Christian Sexuality."
11. Cf. Philippe Delhaye, "Conscience and Church Authority," *Louvain Studies*, Fall, 1969, p. 369: "With an amazing (for him) sense of juridicism, Newman asserts that the burden of proof lies not upon the magisterium but upon the faithful."
12. Charles E. Curran, "Natural Law and Contemporary Moral Theology," in *Contraception: Authority and Dissent*, ed. Charles E. Curran (New York, 1969) p. 171.

would be primarily interested in the way in which "an authentic Christian person makes his ethical decisions and carries them out. . . . Such a theory would also tend to reject the encyclical's view of man and his generative faculties."[13] Curran notes that such a theory would have to enter the world of material norms, but it would constantly realize the "provisional value of its precepts which are limited by the data at hand."[14] (Granted the importance of not doing the right thing for the wrong reason, it seems to me to be equally important, if not much more so, not to do the wrong thing for the right reason.) Secondly, an approach which stresses personal relationships would tend to argue for contraception in some circumstances. Thirdly, a personalist approach "will definitely affect moral conclusions, especially when such conclusions have been based on the physical structure of the act."[15]

First, I think it necessary to respond that a moral theology which accepts revelation, material negative absolutes, and the doctrine of noncontraception can find much in these premises with which to agree. A theology of sex based on the covenants of religion and marriage is certainly interested in whether the decision-maker responds in a spirit of filial obedience; it is certainly concerned with personal relations, for it condemns various sexual acts as violations of an interpersonal relationship intended by God. I have always thought that the evil of adultery was its violation of the personal commitment of marriage. A covenant theology of sex is personalist likewise in that it stresses the presence (or absence) of a covenant freely entered by morally responsible persons.

Such a theology of sex distinguishes between marital and nonmarital contraception; it condemns the former, because the physical act is a sign of refusal to accept the fulness of the meaning of the marriage act as a renewal of the marriage covenant for better or for worse; at the same time it does not

13. *Ibid.*, p. 175.
14. *Ibid.*
15. *Ibid.*, p. 172.

condemn the same physical act in nonmarital relations, because the meaning of a covenant renewal cannot be present. Such a theology of sex accepts the positive values of a personalist approach, but limits the misapplication of these values by likewise accepting certain material negative norms.

Allow me to develop the example of the key club. Let us suppose that some members of a community decided that they should do something more to build community, something to break down the walls that tended to keep them separate. Reasoning that marital sex helped to overcome the barriers of separateness within a given marriage, they decided that the mutual exchange of marriage partners would be helpful in breaking down similar barriers in their limited community. They knew that their actions were contrary to the accepted norms of society, but they also agreed that only by making their own ethic could they develop as self-determining persons. They agreed to set a time limit of two months of weekends as a first experiment and then to decide on the basis of experience whether or not to continue. They likewise decided that the element of chance was more likely to encourage everyone to be polite and kind to everybody else during the week, and thus decided that the women would put the house keys in a hat and that the men would draw keys for their weekend house partners. Realizing the serious and far-reaching consequences of their experiment, they asked a local pastor noted for his liberal views to bless their undertaking. He wished them well but declined the formal blessing because it might upset the more conservative members of his flock. However, he agreed with them that the older theology which talked about adultery as an injustice to the aggrieved partner was not relevant to a situation in which an enlightened husband and wife both fully waived such rights. He also agreed that their use of contraception made irrelevant the older arguments about illegitimate children. He offered only the suggestion that each weekend couple take a fair amount of time to discuss the experiment with each other and that there should be no compulsion felt to go ahead with sexual intercourse if both individuals involved for some reason did not feel like it. Both suggestions were accepted by the group.

The Catholic proponents of contraception will groan that I have created an absurd parody, a straw man, that they thoroughly condemn such things as these key clubs as adultery and affronts to the dignity of man. However, given the premises on which the dissent from *Humanae Vitae* is based, is it not possible that couples could arrive at such a conclusion? To put it in stronger terms, is it possible to avoid such a conclusion?

First, our group's conclusion accepts the premise that there are no absolute material negative norms or that, if there are, they are in doubt. The group has likewise accepted the theological position that the burden of proof "is increasingly upon the ethician to prove and not merely accept as a fact that sexual actuations have meaning only in terms of the marital act."[16] Our group's members cannot see how the older approaches are really relevant and they are not aware of any new approaches that seek to defend the traditional prohibition of such behavior as adultery. The "authorities" were wrong on usury and religious liberty, were they not, and they had to learn from the experience of people, did they not? So our group concludes that the older authorities are equally wrong about sexual liberty and will have to learn from the experience of the people. Then our group has believed itself to be responsible in the way in which they arrived at their decision. They have been open to change, open to each other; they are using the inductive approach of the sciences in their limited experience; they humbly admit that they may possibly be wrong and thus have arranged for an evaluation. They are convinced, therefore, that thus they fulfill the requirements of the transcendental methodology. As for the relational approach, they are convinced that their primary and perhaps even sole purpose is to build and reinforce their community relationships. Certainly they believe they are exercising the new personalism, which calls them to create their

16. *Ibid.*, p. 165.

own decisions, to become truly free. They have looked with respect to the older teaching about adultery but have not been convinced that such guidelines are meaningful for themselves in their situation, which calls for new efforts to build community in a country which is quickly becoming polarized and divided.

Can anything really be said against this if the premises of dissent are granted in the way in which they are proposed and used in some of the contemporary criticism and denial of the doctrine of noncontraception? How does such a picture differ in essence from that presented in a recent novel, in which the hero and heroine, both unmarried, have intercourse one night and receive Holy Communion in St. Peter's the next day, to show their liberation from the old prohibitive Catholic moral teaching? Nor can it be said that such events as key clubs do not exist. They do exist, although the rationale forming them may not be as sophisticated as that of the radical personalism I have illustrated.

I think that much can be said against the position advanced, but not on the basis of the premises of the current authors of dissent. A covenant theology of sex will admit that it can rarely if ever explain in a fully adequate manner the evil of adultery. It can go further and stress the notion of fidelity to God's command and to the personal and irrevocable commitment of marriage. It can point inductively to a consensus among novelists and other writers that the sexual acts condemned by the traditional Catholic morality do not lead to the personal enrichment of those who practice them. Such a covenant theology would have to admit that key clubs were not expressly dealt with by Scripture, but it would not on that account refrain from judging them as adulterous.

A covenant theology of sex will also use the inductive method in questioning the environment in which the new sexual morality has developed. The sexual experience of Scandinavia cannot be ignored; the full personal liberty that has led to the popular current live stage shows of copulation in New York and Los

Angeles cannot be dismissed as irrelevant.[17] Nor can the proposal of the Presbyterians be ignored. It is part of the inductive
evidence showing where the premises of radical personalism
inevitably lead. Its inductive approach would also point to the
fact that modern man today shows a growing acceptance of
the fact that he must learn to live in conformity with nature.
The statement that "modern man could never tolerate a theory
which equates human happiness with conformity to nature"
certainly needs to be modified by the interest modern man is
showing in ecology.[18] The entire body of attack on "physicalism"
in moral theology needs to be re-evaluated in the light of our
understanding that, in the words of the environmentalist, "nature
bats last."

IV

In this whole question of responsibility and dissent, one
huge and primary question keeps coming to mind: "Why bother
at all? Why make this fuss about sexual doctrine and practice?
Why not just tell everybody to do what comes naturally?
Maybe through such an experience we will find out that the
entire biblical and traditional doctrine has no more meaning
for man today than St. Paul's discourse on women's head
coverings. Why should we not accept a radical personalism
in which the sole criterion is 'as long as no one gets hurt, as
long as you don't exploit'?"

Two sets of evidence prevent me from accepting such a
point of view — one is inductive, the other more deductive.
The more inductive evidence comes from contemporary literature. To paraphrase the Walter Lippmann of 1929, the prophets
of a purely personal sex ethic have advocated it, have experienced it, have written about it, and have told us that they

17. *Time,* Nov. 16, 1970, p. 92.
18. Charles E. Curran, "Absolute Norms and Medical Ethics," in *Absolutes in Moral Theology,* ed. Charles E. Curran (Washington, D.C., 1968) p. 122.

have discovered a wasteland.[19] More recently Albert Camus noted in *The Fall* that modern man's history could be written briefly: he fornicated and he read the newspapers. John Updike's recent novel *The Couples*, on suburban adultery, hardly shows the couples enriched. Aldous Huxley in *Brave New World* shows complete sexual satisfaction as one of the primary sources of alienation from within the person. I am not aware of major writers who show their characters more humanized by their sexual liberties. In short, in neither my personal nor my vicarious experience have I found that the sex life that is open to the advocates of radical personalism makes for a more authentic human existence.

The second, more deductive, and more fundamental fact is my acceptance of Christ as the norm of what it means to become fully human. For reasons that I cannot adequately explain, He taught a rigorous doctrine about adultery. I can only conclude that man becomes more human by refusing the temptation of adultery, even when it is only in his mind. The same holds true in my belief for the rest of the sexual doctrine enunciated in Scripture and/or carried to our times by tradition (thus excluding acceptance of an emphasis on the procreative aspect as the *only* value of sex).

If it is true that the person becomes more human by fidelity to the Christian religious covenant and its sexual doctrine, then it is also true that those who advocate a rationale which leads people away from that covenant fidelity must bear a heavy responsibility for the dehumanizing of their listeners and followers.

V

To begin a conclusion, I restate my agreement with Milhaven that the proponents of dissent from the doctrine of non-

---

19. Walter Lippmann, *A Preface to Morals* (New York, 1929). Chapter 14, "Love in the Great Society," is reprinted in slightly abridged form in *Contemporary Moral Values*, ed. H. K. Girvetz (Belmont, Calif., 1968) pp. 296-309.

contraception have presnted a rationale of change which likewise removes the rationale behind the general traditional sexual
doctrine of the Church. I submit that the combination of no
absolutes (either outright denial or extreme reluctance to accept)
and what I have called radical personalism (with its associated
approaches) as used by the current advocates of contraception
and dissent must logically lead to the same attitude with regard
to every other aspect of sexual morality: the tradition perhaps
presents an ideal for ideal people in ideal circumstances, but
in the sinful world in which we live there are no universally
binding material norms. In the last analysis everything is up
to the individual's practical judgment — technically, moral nominalism.

Thus the advocates of contraception present us not only
with a changed doctrine of birth control but implicitly and
logically with an entire package. It is in vain that some might
aver that they hold to the traditional doctrine regarding pre-
marital and extramarital sex, nongenital relations, etc. The fact
that some *will* to hold onto the tradition in some areas while
advocating a different approach in birth control is immaterial.
The logic of their radical personalism marches inexorably. Thus
the doctrine in the body of the recent Presbyterian report comes
as no surprise. I believe it to be unchristian and unecumenical,
but at least it is logical in terms of the premises of radical
personalism.

Certainly my view of this is neither unique nor new. Walter
Lippmann, writing in 1929, attributed the breakdown in sexual
morality to one thing: efficient contraception.[20] He saw it
relieve the fear of pregnancy and thus open the door to all sorts
of sexual activity previously avoided. As previously mentioned,
Charles Curran has accurately noted that the premises of certain
approaches lead to the contraceptive conclusion.

For the various reasons mentioned previously, it is impossible for me at this time to agree that the dissent from *Humanae
Vitae* thus far has been an exercise of responsible loyalty to

---

20. *Ibid.*

the Church. First, the dissent of which I am aware has treated the two sides of the question with different criteria. *Humanae Vitae* is criticized for its reliance on the authority of tradition, while the references to the PBCC are nothing more than repeated appeals to authority. The philosophy of *Humanae Vitae* is severely criticized; the philosophizing of the majority position is generally passed over in polite silence; the dogmatic note of "noninfallible" is emphasized in a way not at all paralleled in the treatment of the social encyclicals. Secondly, the attacks on the philosophizing of *Humanae Vitae* have tended to leave the impression that Christian morality is a matter of philosophical ethics. Thirdly, the advocates of contraception have dissented from *Humanae Vitae* largely on grounds of radical personalism, which leads inexorably to an ethic of moral nominalism: no absolutes, just guidelines suggested for most-of-the-time behavior.

However, little is to be gained from speculation about whether the dissent up to now has been responsible and loyal. More important is the future. It seems to me that the time has come for re-evaluation of the course of dissent.

First, such a re-evaluation needs to consider the proposal of the Presbyterian report on sexual ethics and also the various statements on abortion by various Protestant church bodies of social concern. Are not such statements the direct and inevitable result of denying material absolutes and emphasizing personalism? And is there anything at all that logically stands in the way of advocating complete "liberty"?

Secondly, does not such a re-evaluation need to consider the huge spiritual malaise that has descended upon Western civilization contemporaneous with the ascent of situation ethics, radical personalism, and radical sexual freedom? Is it unreasonable to take into account the high suicide rates of the Scandinavian countries, whose people enjoy full sexual freedom and the highest social security?

One of the more interesting arguments for contraception holds up the principle of the family good and states that contraception may be used to foster the love and good of the entire family.[21] Yet in the face of a society which has had an increasing rate of contraception, we likewise have had a high and increasing rate of divorce. This does not necessarily mean that the use of contraception has been a causal factor in the divorce rate, but it does lead one to question how helpful contraception has been for the authentic good of the family. That is, if it really promoted the family good, could we not expect to see a decrease in the divorce rate as contraception became as widely practiced as it is today?

Thirdly, does not such a re-evaluation need to take a new look at the way in which suffering has been treated? Underlying the whole doctrine of contraception from the 1930 Lambeth Conference to the present is the premise that the suffering of abstinence, especially for long periods, cannot be called for in Christian marriage. (Of course, the logical consequence of such reasoning is that in cases of unavoidable marital abstinence, e.g., severe sickness, separation, etc., extramarital relations become permissible. This reasoning is seen rather clearly in the Presbyterian report.) I want to raise the question of the use of such suffering, voluntarily accepted, in the coredemption of the world. Are not Christians called to suffer with Christ in the redemption of the human race? If so, is there any situation in which we can more normally expect some amount of suffering than in Christian marriage, which as a sacrament is precisely the visible sign, the visible re-enactment, of Christ's redeeming, suffering love for His Church? I see no good in suffering as such, but my Christian faith teaches me that much good has come through suffering willingly accepted in faithful obedience to the Father's call. Furthermore, within marriage, that suffering which is endured because of fidelity to the moral teaching of the Church is especially like Christ's, in that it could be avoided by another course of action and is accepted and endured only through the spirit of faithful obedience to the will of the Father.

___

21. Farrelly, *art. cit.*

In the same light, such a re-evaluation of the theology of dissent needs to reflect on the fact that the absolutizing of the goal of nonsuffering has not only been greatly responsible for the advocacy of contraception but has likewise been greatly influential — perhaps the single greatest influence — in the call for abortion on demand. The modern frame of mind has absolutized nonsuffering. The Planned Parenthood Association, which formerly was somewhat emphatic in its distinction between contraception and abortion (because abortion involved killing a human being), is now silent on such a distinction and advocates abortion as another means of birth control. How can the inductive approach advocated by the theologians of dissent fail to give heavy weight to these phenomena of the modern mind?

Finally, will not such a re-evaluation have to face up to the fact that liberal Christian ethics is in a position similar to liberal Protestant dogmatics, when Karl Barth ascended his pulpit one day and discovered that he really had nothing to say to his people?

Considering the results that have come about already from the development of these modern premises, and considering that such premises seem to form the primary bases for dissent, is continued dissent from the doctrine of marital noncontraception any longer an exercise in responsibility and loyalty to the Church? Has not the time come for the theologians of dissent to do that which they have demanded of the papal magisterium: admit that their premises have been incomplete, their applications faulty, and their conclusions invalid?

Such an admission will not be the end of moral theology. It may well be the beginning of an authentic renewal of a moral theology based on covenant relations. Somehow I have difficulty in equating renewal with the adoption of liberal Protestant and humanist ethics. Readmission of universal negatives may well provide the stimulus for incisive thinking, for perhaps deepening our understanding of what is really forbidden by God in our interpersonal relations. The admission of the importance of the material structure of the human act can be both a help and a stimulus in clarifying and perhaps narrowing the human act involved. A covenant theology of sex which accepts moral absolutes will inevitably encounter problems, but I remain convinced at present that it offers far greater promise than that of a radical personalism. I will gladly accept the criticism of those who can show me that my fears are unfounded, that the personalism that leads to contraception does not also go the rest of the way of the Presbyterian report — and further; but considering the inductive evidence available already in liberal Protestant ethics, I hope I may be pardoned for saying that I am not holding my breath.

APPENDIX III

CATHOLIC SEXUAL ETHICS:
THE CONTINUING DEBATE ON BIRTH CONTROL

John F. Kippley

Reprinted by permission from the *Linacre Quarterly*, February 1974, the official publication of the National Federation of Catholic Physicians' Guilds, 2825 N. Mayfair Road, Milwaukee, Wisconsin, 53222.

Introduction: The Present Situation

The fifth anniversary of the promulgation of *Humanae Vitae* has passed without tremendous fanfare, but the little notice that was taken may be significant. Father Richard McCormick, S.J. called attention to the silence since *Humanae Vitae* on the part of the local magisterium.[1] Suggesting that this silence and the statistics of massive dissent are themselves new theological data, he called for a Blue Ribbon Commission to re-study the matter; his hope was clearly that such a Commission would come up with a revision of *Humanae Vitae* that would state a general preferred practice but leave the door open for contraception where the couple felt a conflict of values. Concerning this silence, Ms. Karen Hurley, a married woman with an advanced degree in theology, recommended that it be halted and that the challenge of *Humanae Vitae* be once again presented.[2]

---

1. See in-journal article, p. 26.
2. Hurley, Karen, "Birth Control: Let's End the Silence," *St. Anthony Messenger*, October, 1973, pp. 10-15.

If the voice of support for this doctrine of marital non-contraception has been largely unheard, the voice of dissent has certainly filled the vacuum at every level. In most cities and towns it is common knowledge that there are priests who will aid the decision to practice contraception. Perhaps it is less commonly known that many of our high school students are taught to dissent from *Humanae Vitae* and are thus oriented towards contraception practically from the onset of puberty. A college freshman recently told me that when she was in the ninth grade (1969-70), the priest teaching religion in her Catholic high school had effectively taught her class to dissent. "Here's what the Pope said, but here's what all the theologians say." Thus, as she put it, all of her friends who were now marrying were going on the Pill without the slightest thought that this was contrary to the official moral teaching of the Church. She declined to name the high school because, as she put it, "It doesn't make much difference. My friends from other Catholic schools got the same message."

Nor is the state of the question limited to contraception. Recurrent surveys indicate that there has been a similar dissent from the Church's official teaching on abortion and non-marital coitus. For example, McCready and Greeley have reported that among Catholics under 30, 36% saw premarital intercourse as not wrong at all, and 35% saw it as wrong only sometimes.[3] A Gallup poll a year later reported that 45% of the Roman Catholics interviewed "categorized pre-marital sex as 'not wrong.' The figures for Protestants was 38%. The 1969 figures were 16% for Catholics and 20% for Protestants."[4]

With regard to abortion, McCready and Greeley reported, among other things, that 74% of the Catholics under 30 would allow abortion if there was a strong chance of a serious birth defect in the baby. That is an interesting parallel with the finding of Bumpass-Westhoff that 75% of Catholics under 30

3. McCready, William C. and Greeley, Andrew M., "The End of American Catholicism?" *America*. October 28, 1972, p. 335.
4. *National Observer*, August 25, 1973, p. 15.

were using birth control methods disapproved by the Church.[5] I submit that it is almost unimaginable that a Catholic not using contraception on moral grounds could then approve of killing nascent life. Thus, if our professional sociologists' surveys are valid and reliable, I submit that we have a most visible indication of the real link between contraception and abortion no matter how different these realities are. The above surveys would indicate a correlation of close to 100% between the acceptance of contraception and the acceptance of quality-of-life abortion among the people surveyed.

This, then, is the situation as we head into the second five year period post-*Humanae Vitae*. On the one hand, a challenge has been thrown to our bishops to validate the dissenting theory and practice; on the other hand the bishops are faced with repeated evidences of crisis and decline within the Church in the decade that has seen a majority of Catholics accept the contraceptive way of life. They can hardly ignore the above mentioned relationships between dissent from the doctrine of marital non-contraception and the dissent in the matters of abortion and overall sexual doctrine.

The situation is considerably changed from that of 1968 in that dissent and the dissenters have been riding high in the saddle in practically every area of Catholic life for the past five years and for much of the past decade. As such, they have established a track record, and, in a day when consequentialism is much in vogue among moralists, this is certainly strong theological data. Thus, whether one considers the relative silence by the magisterium and the majority acceptance of contraception by some as the point of emphasis in calling for a reconsideration of *Humanae Vitae* or whether one thinks that dissent vis-a-vis abortion and overall sexuality necessitates a hard look at the acceptance of dissent and contraception, there are three outstanding facts. The debate about contraception should not be allowed to die, some further authoritative teaching is called for and the relative silence should not continue for another five years.

---

5. Quoted by McCormick, *op. cit.*

If it is valid to call for a reconsideration of *Humanae Vitae*, then it is equally valid to call for a reconsideration of the dissent. To that end, I propose in this article to provide 1) a relatively brief and selective critique of the document of dissent from the *Catholic Hospital Directives* and 2) an analysis of the major lines of reasoning for the acceptance of contraception. In providing such analyses, I realize that I speak from a minority position and that thus a majority of my potential readership has already taken an opposite position. The difficulty is compounded because in this task I am opposing the rationale of those who are rightly called "eminent scholars."[6]

By way of ameliorating this initial handicap, I would ask consideration of two factors. First of all, the document of dissent from the *Hospital Directives* was to be expected. After all, if a large number of theologians have taken a stance against *Humanae Vitae* and then are confronted by *Directives* which put *Humanae Vitae* into practice, it is predictable that a certain number of theologians would issue a statement of dissent from such *Directives*. It is also quite understandable why they should choose to operate as a study commission of the Catholic Theological Society of America, for such a platform assures a promulgation of their views to some of the most influential people in theology today.

Secondly, however, the Commission members called attention to the fact that "the obvious theoretical limit to legitimate dissent is the truth itself *as expressed in the reasons for the dissent from a particular teaching.*"[7] Thus they ask us not to accept their dissent stance on the basis of faith in their scholarship but rather on the basis of the reasons they put forth. Thus they would be the first to invite a rational dissent from their own position, and this is what I hope to provide.

In the first section of what follows I shall attempt to show that dissent from the *Directives* is not justified on the very

---

6. Editorial introduction to the "Report of the Commission on Ethical and Religious Directives for Catholic Hospitals," *Linacre Quarterly.* November, 1972, p. 246.
7. CTSA Commission Report, para. 64, emphasis mine.

grounds that are put forth by the dissenters in the CTSA Commission Report; in the second section I shall attempt to uphold a similar position with regard to the dissent from *Humanae Vitae*.

I. A Selective Critique of the CTSA Commission Report

It is not feasible to offer a commentary on the entire CTSA Commission Report (hereafter, the *Report*) which is about 6000 words in length. Thus my comments are limited to 1) three rather general reasons that form a framework for dissent, and 2) the four specific conditions listed as justifying noncompliance with the *Directives*.

A. The ecumenical dimension of Catholic sexual ethics.

Upon the issuance of *Humanae Vitae* it was rather widely stated that the encyclical was definitely a snag in the ecumenical dialogue. This theme has understandably been picked up in the dissent from the *Directives*: no one can deny that refusal by a Catholic hospital to allow certain actions that neither a Protestant patient nor doctor find objectionable may very well lead to negative feelings on their part toward the Catholic church. (On the other hand, they might admire a stand on principle, particularly in the aftermath of the Watergate principals and principles.) Thus the *Report* noted that "the Decree on Ecumenism affirms the ecclesial reality of other churches and the possibility of learning from the theological and ethical insights developed within other Christian communities" (para. 15).

Within the context of the *Report* and the overall debate, this has the effect of saying two things: 1) perhaps the Protestants are right and the Catholic magisterium is wrong about the sexual matters under debate; 2) at the least, we Catholics shouldn't stand in the way of letting people of good faith use Catholic hospital facilities as they see fit.

The problem with such a stance is that it provides a formal approach that provides no firm basis for refusing abortion facilities to such people of good faith. That is, if it is argued that good faith and perhaps a statement of a Christian Church are sufficient criteria on the grounds of ecumenism not to prohibit one type of behavior, then under *that* formality other types of behavior would also have to be admitted. If on the other hand it is said to the non-Catholic (or dissenting Catholic), "You can't use our facilities for abortion because *we* believe that it is a morally evil action even if you don't see it that way," we Catholics can once again be accused of having introduced an ecumenical snag and of not really respecting the ethical insights of the various Protestant and Jewish communities that have strongly supported a woman's right to abortion for almost any reason. Considering that most of the larger Protestant church bodies in the United States have issued some sort of statement favoring the women's right for a quality-of-life abortion, there is practically as much of an ecumenical impasse on that issue as there is on that of the formal teaching about contraception. Thus, dissent from the *Directives* on the grounds of ecumenism is not well founded unless the dissenters are prepared to admit abortion and other actions that are now or may be issues of separation.

B. The grounds of emergency care.

"Medical or surgical treatment may be morally permissible in an emergency situation where a delay might involve grave risks, while the same type of treatment may be excluded in elective situations" (para. 58).

I fail to see the value of this statement as a grounds for dissent because the dissent from the *Directives* is principally concerned with matters related to human sexuality and generation. Aside from a last-minute craniotomy, aren't these other matters elective? It may be more convenient to perform a tubal ligation at the time of a caesarian, but it is still elective; thus the *Catholic Hospital Directives* do not deprive a person of any medically necessary care. Rather they protect the patient from the vagaries of what is socially acceptable elective medical practice, not a bad idea considering the history of acceptability among the German medical profession in the 1930's and the now well known, pro-abortion-via-a-new-ethic editorial in *California Medicine*.[8]

C. Non-infallible because concrete.

In paragraph 63 of the *Report*, potential decision makers are told that they may "licitly act contrary to the concrete (*and hence non-infallible*) ethical directives" on four conditions. (Emphasis mine.) According to this statement, any ethical directive is non-infallible *simply because it is concrete.* Earlier, (para. 44) the *Report* had stated the urgency of "a general, but clear and firm policy of exclusion of abortion on the part of Catholic health institutions." However, such a policy can be criticized not only as being unecumenical, but such critics could also point out that the Catholic dissenters have themselves stated that any ban on abortion must be non-infallible simply because it is a very concrete directive.

Note well what is happening. Dissent is theoretically based on the fact that *Humanae Vitae* was not promulgated in a *de fide* form; but then the dissenters go further and deny that *any* concrete directive can be infallible. Thus, there can be no universal concrete norms. Therefore, should Pope or Council at some time declare against abortion, or contraception or some other moral matter in a *de fide* form, our dissenters have already set the stage to dissent from *that*. Let us be aware of the full implications of the parenthetical phrasing, and let at least one voice be counted against such a universal prohibition of universal moral norms.

D. The four conditions necessary for non-compliance with the *Directives* (para. 63)

1. "Good conscience after careful reflection." No one is going to argue with the necessity of there being a good conscience on the part of one who would dissent from the teaching of the Church. At the same time, everyone will admit that this is something that only God can judge. Of itself, it offers

---

8. *California Medicine*, September, 1970.

no help in framing directives for the Catholic hospital, for good conscience is assumed on the part of those who would practice abortion and euthanasia as well as those who would practice surgical sterilization, etc. Considering the appeal of the Eichmanns and the Calleys of history to the goodness of their consciences, the fact of "good conscience" provides no assurance that grave evil will not be done.

2. Openmindedness. The second condition for non-compliance with the *Directives* is that the dissenting parties must have paid "respectful and openminded attention to the authoritative teaching of the hierarchy as well as other sources of moral wisdom in the light of the Gospel." The same comments that applied to the condition of good conscience also apply here: only God can judge such open-mindedness; if it is claimed, it cannot be either verified or disapproved. From a practical viewpoint it is of little help in an age of conflicting wisdoms. Should a Catholic hospital really allow or tolerate the practice of infanticide of defective babies by those who in good conscience were persuaded by the wisdom of Dr. Watson's suggestion of a three day trial observation before a newborn child would be given legal and moral rights as a human being?

3. No undue harm to third parties. The third condition for allowing non-compliance would require that "no undue harm" be done to the "life, well-being or rights of a third party." Here at least the criteria seems to be more tangible, something objective as contrasted with the inherent subjectivism of the previous conditions. However, closer analysis reveals that the terminology of no "undue" harm offers little help in clarifying the grounds for dissent. The question is immediately raised, "Who is to judge whether a certain physical action is 'undue' harm?" What if a member of a hospital psychiatric clinic wanted to practice "therapeutic coitus" with a patient and had his or her spouse's consent? And does not the whole abortion debate center around whether it is "undue harm" to the unborn child? Suppose that a Catholic woman and her Jewish doctor want to have an abortion performed and that they have a Protestant theologian's counsel for that abortion? Faced with the CTSA

Report's emphasis on religious liberty, the fallibility of all moral directives and dissent, one wonders how a Catholic hospital could long maintain a non-abortion policy. What judge, given the CTSA Report as reliable interpretation of Catholic doctrine, could refrain, from issuing a court order compelling the hospital to allow abortions just as they have done with regard to sterilization? And is this not especially true in the light of the Supreme Court decision that no undue harm can be done to a third person in the first six months because the baby is not defined as a person entitled to legal protection? Part I of the CTSA Commission Report needs to be re-read in the light of the Supreme Court decision on abortion. Eleven and a half of that section's thirteen paragraphs provide a ready made case for anyone who wanted to force Catholic hospitals to be no different from any other hospital. Certainly a proviso against "undue harm" to third parties speaks well for the intentions of the framers of the Report: my problem with it is that it seems to do little at the practical level to carry out that good intention. Rather, the debate that is immediately raised by such terminology helps to establish the necessity of the concreteness of the *Directives*.

4. The avoidance of scandal. The last criteria for dissent is that scandal be avoided. "This last condition means that precautions must be taken to prevent this exception from causing more harm than good..." I submit that with the present state of both informal and formal communications networks, there is no way that interested people are not going to know what is going on in the Catholic hospital. Furthermore there will not be "exceptions" but only "first cases." Allow one contraceptive sterilization, artificial insemination, etc. and on what grounds do you refuse another in these days of court orders?

In an age where good conscience and the wisdoms of our day are used to justify anything and everything, when there is widespread disagreement about whether killing an unborn child is an "undue harm," the first three conditions offer no significant material barrier to almost any imaginable physical actuation, and, as we have just seen, there is no way in which the fourth condition can be fulfilled. If the question were one of simply avoiding personal culpability while acting contrary to God's order of creation, then the four conditions would be helpful as applied to various actions taking place in hospitals and clinics in no way associated with the Catholic church. However, the legitimate teaching authority of the Church is called upon to teach what is right and wrong, rather than the grounds for non-culpability. Where it is practically possible for this teaching authority to prevent certain objective wrongs from being done, it is obliged to do so. Thus, the bishops are under a moral obligation to direct Catholic hospitals not to allow certain actions to be performed regardless of the subjective state or conscience of those who would perform them. The conditions that the Report offers for non-compliance may serve well to insure moral non-culpability for that action done elsewhere, but they do not provide any sufficient grounds for the Catholic hospital to allow such non-compliance within its jurisdiction.

II. A Limited Critique of the Bases for Dissent

As mentioned previously, the Report was a predictable document because it is quite reasonable for those who dissent from the doctrine of *Humanae Vitae* to spell out their consequent dissent from the *Directives* which seek to put *Humanae Vitae* into practice in Catholic hospitals. Though I think that the dissenters have erred in both cases, it is to their credit that they have explicitly stated "beyond the four conditions mentioned," there is an "obvious theoretical limit to legitimate dissent," namely "the truth itself as expressed in the reasons for the dissent from a particular teaching" (para. 64). Not all statements of dissent have admitted this limitation. Thus, even *if* the four conditions had been sufficent for justifying non-compliance with the *Directives,* such non-compliance would still be illegitimate if the reasons given for dissent from *Humanae Vitae* were seen to be insufficient, inadequate, or lacking in the truth. In this attempt to show the invalidity of the reasons given for dissent, I shall follow somewhat of an historical approach beginning with the Majority Report of the Papal Birth Control Commission and concluding with the present stage of arguments.

A. A Theory of Partial Acts.

The Majority Report took the position that individual acts of coitus within marriage are only partial acts. The contraceptive acts were seen to be justified by reference to the non-contraceptive acts. "This is the case for matrimonial acts which are composed of several fertile and (contraceptively) infertile acts; they constitute one totality because they are referred to one deliberate choice."[9]

Despite the prestige of its authors, this line of reason has failed to win much support. It has not proved to be intellectually convincing, probably because of the ease with which it can be criticized.

1. If the individual sex act is an incomplete act whose morality is taken from the whole, the *individual* sex act becomes morally insignificant. If that is so, it is difficult to account for the concern that men of all ages — both Christian and non-Christian — have had about the morality of individual acts of sexual intercourse. Again, if the morality of individual sex acts is to be evaluated only in terms of the overall marriage and not in themselves then, of course, nothing serious can be said against individual acts of anal or oral intercourse, or, for that matter, against individual acts of intercourse with other persons if this was done with the marriage partner's consent. The majority position paper attempted to respond to these criticisms raised by the minority position, but it offered no logical and consistent reason for its rejection of oral or anal intercourse. When it stated that "in these acts there is preserved neither the dignity of love nor the dignity of the spouse as human persons created according to the image of God,"[10] the

---

9. As quoted in *The Birth Control Debate*, Robert G. Hoyt, ed. Kansas City, Mo: National Catholic Reporter, 1968 p,. 72.
10. *Ibid.*

position of Fuchs *et al.* was simply not answering the question but rather stating the faith or opinions of its authors. It did not teach us *why* such actions are contrary to the dignity of man; nor did it teach us why these acts *contra dignitatem* were not morally insignificant and why they should not be seen simply as partial acts whose morality is taken from the overall totality of sexual acts in that marriage. Any theory which seeks to justify marital contraception or sterilization in terms of the totality of the marriage simply has to come to grips with the objection based on these acts of non-vaginal intercourse. If it condemns them as perverse, it has to explain why (and why they are not just "partial"); if it allows them, then in all honesty the proponents of such a theory should make it clear to their readers or followers that their permission of contraception also includes permission of these other forms of intercourse.

2. Secondly, operating within a Catholic context, it becomes necessary to explain how one's theory of permitting contraception accords with the doctrine of Vatican II that "the moral aspect of any procedure (of birth regulation) does not depend solely on sincere intentions or on an evaluation of motives. It must be determined by objective standards. These, based on the nature of the human person and his acts, preserve the full sense of mutual self-giving and human procreation in the context of true love. Such a goal cannot be achieved unless the virtue of conjugal chastity is sincerely practiced."[11] The majority paper attempted to reconcile its position with this statement and arrived at a mixture of subjectivism and efficiency which I have analyzed elsewhere.[12] Reviewing my analysis of the majority position. Robert Dailey, S.J. noted that it "shows the weaknesses in the criteria proposed by the majority report of the papal commission — weaknesses which even the most sympathetic supporters of that opinion have puzzled over."[13]

---

11. *Gaudium et Spes*, para. 51.
12. Kippley, John F., *Covenant, Christ and Contraception*, Staten Island: Alba House, 1970, pp. 91-92.
13. Dailey, Robert H., S.J., "Book Review Section," *Theological Studies*, 1971, 32, June, p. 344.

There have been many references to the Majority Report by those who have favored dissent; however, in almost every instance, these references have been to the Report as to an "authority" rather than to the reasons given. I submit that this is an excellent indication that the dissenters themselves have, in all honesty, failed to be convinced by the reasoning that was supposed to convince the Pope.

B. A Theory of Personal Judgment.

When the Minority Report raised its objection that to admit contraception was to grant liceity to anal and oral intercourse, it was not kindly received. The authors of those objections seemed to be regarded by the vocal Catholic world at the time as being traditionalists out of touch with reality.

No such label can be applied to revisionist[14] theologian Michael Valenti. According to this theory, what makes man in the image and likeness of God is his rationality.[15] Using his reason and not bound by a static concept of nature, he will come to know what is right and wrong.

For Valenti, "sex is personal. Consequently its morality must be subject to the highly personal judgment of the individual . . . Subject to reason, to an understanding of the consequences of actions, and to a commitment to responsibility; and performed in harmony with the purposes of human life, any sexual act takes its morality . . . whether it be a moral evaluation of good or evil — from individual circumstances and individual intention."[16]

Those conditions could be the subject of an extended debate, but fortunately Valenti does not leave us in a cloud of vagueness. "The case of bestiality provides an interesting example. The individual who finds sexual release in bestiality has carried the masturbatory model into the area of animal affection . . . Denied such activity, he might never progress beyond wishing

14. Valenti, Michael F., Sex: The Radical View of a Catholic Theologian, New York: Bruce, 1970, p. 16.
15. Ibid., p. 22.
16. Ibid., p. 135.

for it. Permitted, he might indeed progress beyond it. But, in any case, where is the harm in it?"[17] He also notes that it seems unreasonable to make a moral distinction between allowing the use of a condom and anal intercourse, or coitus interruptus, masturbation, and homosexuality.[18] In addition, "if the use of sexuality outside the married state is to be forbidden, it must be forbidden on grounds apart from the natural law doctrine."[19]

Scriptural dicta might seem to offer some real impediments to such a theology. However, Professor Valenti finds no problem. They are "simply the expressions of the author's convictions as to how everyday problems of living must be resolved in accordance with the thrust of the Judaic-Christian ethical message."[20] Thus their prohibitions against fornication, adultery, sodomy — in all its senses, and bestiality do not reflect the divine order of creation. Presumably this would also apply to the teaching of Jesus as well.

The theory of Valenti has received scant attention from his fellow revisionists perhaps because of the truly radical approach he has developed. Such relative silence would seem to suggest that they think he has erred. However, if he is in error, it is on one of two points: either his initial premises are wrong or he has erred in his logic in drawing out his conclusions. In my estimation, he has correctly spelled out his conclusions, and thus the error lies at the heart of the strongest position of dissent: the acceptance of the liceity of contraception.

C. A third approach has been developed by such men as Peter Chirico, S.S., Charles Robert, Peter Knauer, S.J., and Bruno Schuller, S.J. in the context of moral conflict. Richard McCormick has summarized some key elements of their thought.[21] While agreeing with their conclusions in favor of

17. *Ibid.*, p. 140.
18. *Ibid.*, p. 126.
19. *Ibid.*
20. *Ibid.*, p. 147.
21. McCormick, Richard, S.J., "Notes on Moral Theology," *Theological Studies*, 32, March, 1971 pp. 88-97.

rejecting the key doctrine of *Humanae Vitae*[22] he is not entirely happy with their reasoning.[23] This approach grants that contraception is a physical evil but asks "when and how does physical evil become moral evil?"[24] The answer, "when it occurs without proportionate cause" of course raises the question of proportionality and the problem of "proportionate in whose mind?" The authors are not unaware of the dangers of a total relativism, nor do they confine their approach only to contraception and sterilization; abortion and other forms of killing are also very much a part of the discussion.

Basically, this approach centers on the conflict of values and denies the validity of any universal rules of behavior, e.g., "never engage in marital contraception or contraceptive sterilization," "never directly kill an innocent person." Despite disclaimers,[25] it is very difficult to see the difference between this and a situation ethic, one of whose basic rules is "never say never."

In order to try to prevent this approach from becoming a de facto situation ethic or ethic of intentionalism it is stressed that there must be a proportionate or commensurate reason for causing the physical evil. "For Knauer, a reason is commensurate if the manner of the present achievement of a value will not undermine but support the value in the long run and in the whole picture. This is a sound description of proportionality. But who can confidently make such a judgment? An individual? Hardly."[26] There is not only a conflict of values involved in this question; there is also a conflict of interest. Under the influences of various factors that incline them towards contraception and unlimited coitus, what individuals or couples can say that their practice of contraception or sterilization is going to do more to further respect for sex, marriage, their own relationship, and life itself, than the practice of

22. *Ibid.*, p. 83.
23. *Ibid.*, pp. 83, 94.
24. *Ibid.*, p. 92.
25. *Ibid.*
26. *Ibid.*, p. 94.

periodic continence? McCormick notes that this problem shows the need for a larger perspective, that of "scientific moral theology and the desirability of a magisterium."[27]

No one can doubt the appeal of this approach. It avoids the pitfalls of the partial act theory and at first glance it appears to avoid the radical individualism of the personal judgment theory; at least the language is much more couched and there is a recognition of a preferred way or meant-to-be. A further appeal for many Catholic theologians is that this approach allows them to say that *Humanae Vitae* was right in providing a theoretical ideal but its error was in making the ideal into a norm or rule.

Certainly this notion of an ideal but not a universally applicable norm, a value that may or must be ceded in the face of conflict with other values has great appeal for the priest who counsels a couple who find themselves having difficulty in living up to the challenging demand of *Humanae Vitae*. He can give the appearance of being not really opposed to the Pope and *Humanae Vitae*, of being theologically up-to-date as he quotes such people as Crotty and Knauer, and of having sympathy for the couple. Because of the stature of the theologians who have adopted this approach and its inherent pastoral appeal, I think that this approach has probably been used by the majority of priests who have abandoned the position actually taken by *Humanae Vitae*.

However, the value of an idea in moral theology is not its appeal based upon its ability to make counseling more comfortable, and this approach has some very serious difficulties.

1. First of all, it might be worthwhile to note that this approach is not a valid interpretation of *Humanae Vitae*. Pope Paul pre-empted it as follows:

"Now, some may ask: in the present case, is it not reasonable in many circumstances to have recourse to artificial birth control if, thereby, we secure the harmony and peace of the family, and better conditions for the education of the children already

---

27. *Ibid.*, p. 95.

born? To this question it is necessary to reply with clarity, the Church is the first to praise and recommend the intervention of intelligence in a function which so closely associates the rational creature with his Creator, but she affirms that this must be done with respect for the order established by God."[28] The Pope then spells out why the use of the infertile period is licit under some circumstances while the use of contraception is not.

2. A second criticism stems directly from the expression of proportionalism stated earlier by Knauer and McCormick: "A reason (for allowing the physical evil of contraception) is commensurate if the manner of the present achievement of a value will not undermine but support the value in the long run and in the whole picture."[29]

How is one to make such a determination of the overall consequences? Prior to the actual consequences, one can only prognosticate. However, since this sort of theorizing has been with us in Catholic theology for some time, and since it has been with us for a longer time in Protestantism, it is now possible to describe the track record.

What sort of values would the acceptance of contraception be trying to further? I would expect no real debate that two values have been seen as being hopefully fostered by contraception: a) the value of marriage and marital happiness; b) the value of sex. Indirectly, through the reduction of the number of originally unwanted children, the acceptance of contraception might also be seen to enhance mankind's overall respect for human life.

a. While it is easy to find people who will say that their practice of contraception has made their marriage easier, I am not aware of any data that purport to show that the acceptance and practice of contraception have really helped to support the value of marriage and marital happiness "in the long run and in the whole picture." Instead, the indications are just the

---

28. *Humanae Vitae,* para. 16.
29. McCormick, *op. cit.,* p. 94.

opposite. Between 1940 and 1967, certainly a time of great increase in the use of contraception, the divorce rates in the United States rose from 165 to 279 per 1000 marriages, an increase of 69%.[30] I would not suggest that the use of contraception is the sole cause of the marital unhappiness indicated by such figures, but I am suggesting that if contraception were the great aid to marital happiness and supporter of the real values of marriage, then it is certainly strange that there has been such a parallel rise of marital unhappiness and breakup concurrent with the increased use of contraceptives.

b. Furthermore, experience has shown that the acceptance of contraception as a means of supporting the value of sex actually undermines the value of sex in the long run and in the whole picture, at least if coitus is considered to be a marital act. Walter Lippmann pointed this out in 1929 when he noted that the logic of contraception opened the door to every kind of sex outside of marriage, to companionate marriages, etc.[31] We have already seen Michael Valenti argue for contraception and point out that its logic cannot say no to any imaginable form of voluntary sexual actuation if the persons involved think it will be helpful. The findings of McCready and Greeley cited in the opening section of this article indicate that a significant majority of the under-30 age group has lifted the ban on pre-marital sex for themselves. This is the generation that has been taught to dissent from the official doctrine on contraception. Their attitudes about sex in general support the view that acceptance of contraception in an effort to promote the values of sex has the reverse effect and leads to an overall lowering of sexual values.

c. In a related area, the value of life itself has been cheapened by the practice of contraception. It is especially troubling

30. Kleiner, Richard H., *Marriage and Family Relationships*, New York: Harper and Row, 1970, p. 20.

31. Lippmann, Walter, "Love in the Great Society," in *Contemporary Moral Issues*, 2nd ed., ed. by Harry K. Girvetz, Belmont, Calif.: Wadsworth, 1969, pp. 299-303. This is a selection from *A Preface to Morals*. New York: Macmillan, 1929, pp. 285-313.

to see the growth in numbers of Catholics who accept abortion consequent upon the growth in the numbers who accepted contraception.[32] All of this should hardly surprise us. St. Thomas pointed out over 700 years ago that action proceeds from virtue and that the moral virtues are inter-connected.[33]

Of course, the proponents of dissent via proportionalism can respond that the time element and the context I have described are really not "in the long run and in the whole picture." I have interpreted this reason for dissent to be speaking of a relatively short (in the history of man) time period, especially in today's mass and rapid communications when the consequences of ideas show up much more quickly than in previous eras. If the proponents of dissent are talking in terms of a century, then it seems to me that they are not providing a reason that can be analyzed but are rather asking for an act of faith, and if we are dealing with contrary acts of faith, I am not aware of a Catholic ecclesiology that could seriously hold for the act of faith in the proponents of dissent in the face of the teaching of the magisterium.

I have also evaluated the consequences of the acceptance of contraception from the point of view of the Catholic tradition which sees non-marital sex, divorce and remarriage, and abortion as disvalues.

Within these contexts, I think that the argument for proportionality fails to be intellectually satisfying on the very grounds quoted earlier from Knauer.

3. A third criticism of the approaches of proportionalism is that they tend to treat the sexual act as *only* a physical act and contraception as *only* a physical evil that becomes a moral evil when done without proportionate reason. However, life is not that simple. The marriage act is a sacred act, a "sacramental" one. It is meant to symbolize the marriage union and

---

32. McCready and Greeley, *op. cit.*, p. 336.
33. *Summa Theologica*, I-II. Q. 65, a. 1.

to renew the marriage covenant. Because it is the specific *marriage* act, the words of Christ are validly applied, "What God has united, man must not divide". (Mark 10:9) The whole meaning of contraception is to take apart the unitive and procreative aspects of marital coitus that God has mysteriously joined together. (It is something entirely different to respect the order of creation and to make use of the times when the Author of nature has allowed the unitive and procreative aspects to be separated.)

4. A fourth and lesser reason for faulting the argument from proportionality in this case as a grounds for dissent either from *Humanae Vitae* or the *Hospital Directives* is the evaluation that Father McCormick made of this line of reasoning. When he concluded to the need of "a scientific moral theology and *the desirability of a magisterium*" (emphasis mine) in order to have a larger perspective and to avoid a radical situation ethic, he certainly offered no reason for dissent: far from that, he in effect offered more support for the acceptance of *Humanae Vitae* and its practical conclusions in hospitals, though that was certainly not his intent.

In all three of these approaches there has been the capital omission of what the formally stated doctrine of the magisterium actually is. Neither Pius XI or Paul VI spoke in terms of simply the physical structure of the sexual act. Note the key statement of *Casti Connubii*: "Any use whatever of marriage, in the exercise of which the act by human effort is deprived of its natural power of procreating life...;" and that of *Humanae Vitae*: "...each and every marriage act (quilibet matrimonii usus) must remain open to the transmission of life." That phrasing is significantly different from "every act of sexual intercourse."

Certainly they had reference to nature, but not simply in the physical sense. The formal documents limit the condemnation of contraception as sinful to those acts which are truly marital. Thus the papal teaching seems to be that marital contraception is a sin against the nature of marriage. (Of course, it can be argued that if the question about non-marital relations were really pressed, the Popes might have responded in a similar manner. I limit myself to the de facto stated doctrine.)

Thus the formal papal doctrine teaches us about the conditions for valid *marital* intercourse. It does not treat of sex in a purely physical way but as an expression of the personal and sacred commitment of marriage. Then at the same time and *because* it recognizes that marriage itself is more than just whatever two people want to say it is (but rather has a divinely created objective order), it likewise teaches that the marriage act has an objective order that must be respected. It is for such reasons that I previously noted that the words of Jesus about marriage itself can be applied to the marriage act: "What God has united, man must not divide." Such considerations are important because much of the procontraceptive theologizing seems to have been based on the false premise that the papal doctrine has been a statement about a physical act without regard to circumstances. (For example, see the proportionality arguments as noted above.) However, "marriage" is the great circumstance in all of Catholic sexual doctrine, and this holds true likewise with regard to contraception. Because it is a sacred act and not just a biological or romantic one, the marriage act may not be tampered with and be deprived of the elements that God has joined together.

Another erroneous assumption that underlies much of the theology of contraception is that Natural Family Planning simply does not work. The Majority Report stated that the rhythm method was very much lacking efficiency and that "only sixty per cent of women have a regular cycle." No criteria for "regular" or "rhythm" was given, thus making the statement not only non-scientific but, taken as a whole, inaccurate and misleading. On the other hand, the placement of the use of the post-ovulatory phase basal temperature method among the "most effective" methods of birth regulation by Dr. Christopher Tietze of the Population Council[34] leads one to think that the writers of the Majority Report were not as fully informed as they might have been. The truth of the matter is that modern Natural Family Planning provides a very efficient control of conception for those who are willing to exercise a modicum of self-control, one of the fruits of the Spirit (Galatians 5:23).

Earlier in this article, I expressed my gratitude that the framers of the dissent from the *Hospital Directives* admitted clearly that any dissent was limited by the actual truth of the reasons given for that dissent. I have tried to show that such truth is lacking and that therefore by their own admission such dissent has become illegitimate. These may seem like strong words, but are they any stronger than those used by the dissenters who have said that the Pope has erred and that his doctrine of sex is invalid?

I am much more hopeful that the theologians of dissent will be open to my criticisms in 1974 than they would have been in 1969. For one thing, I grant them good faith, even if some of them were a bit too anxious to be "with it." I know that many of them must be very concerned about the shape of Catholic thinking as reported by the recent surveys. Secondly, I have seen people, for whom it must have been difficult, announce their new acceptance of *Humanae Vitae* after their association with the popular rejection of it back in 1968. One of these was a well known marriage counselor in the Twin Cities; another was a well known priest and theologian who told a large audience that he had been wrong and Paul VI right; within the last two weeks of writing these words, I have

----

34. Tietze, Christopher, M.D., "Ranking of Contraceptive Methods by Levels of Effectiveness," *Excerpta Medica International Congress Series No.* 224: proceedings of the VIII Annual meeting of the AAAPP, Boston, April 9-10, 1970. In addition to a study by John Marshall, M.D., he cites a multi-authored French study that found one "method failure" in 17,500 cycles.

read a paper by a religious sister and M.D. who told of her change and concluded that Paul VI was exercising the prophetic role and receiving the usual reward. I have reason to believe that a significant factor in these decisions was the observation of the consequences of the acceptance of contraception. Three swallows don't make a spring, but these personal cases confirm other reports I have heard that attitudes are changing.[35]

A fourth reason for my hope that priests, theologians and laity will be more open to my criticisms of the theology of dissent is the growing awareness that compliance with *Humanae Vitae* does not leave them in a hopeless corner with no way out. Natural Family Planning is getting its second wind, so to speak. We know what kind of breastfeeding provides a long period of natural post-partum amenorrhea and infertility; we know how to become aware of the fertile period through mucus and cervix observations; we know how to correlate these signs with the positive basal temperature indication that fertility has passed. Mr. Lawrence Kane of the Human Life Foundation recently told me of a meeting he had with some priests. When he described the present state of the art of Natural Family Planning, one of the priests spoke up, "We wouldn't have joined the dissent movement back in '68 if we knew then what you've just told us."

III. The Role of Catholic Physicians

In the light of the absence of adequate reasons for continued dissent, it would seem that the role of the Catholic physician can be stated both negatively and positively. Negatively, they should neither prescribe contraceptives nor perform contraceptive surgery. They should recognize the definitely possible

---

35. See 1) Klaus, Hanna, M.D., "A Second Look at Humanae Vitae," *Homiletic and Pastoral Review*, October, 1973, pp. 59-67.
2) Riga, Peter, "Humanae Vitae and the New Sexuality," *Triumph*, October, 1973, pp. 18-20.

abortifacient character of the oral contraceptives[36] and the overwhelming evidence that the I.U.D. is an abortifacient,[37] and they should so inform their patients. They should take the time to relate the artificial birth control movement to the abortion movement. They might also relate it to the most recent anti-life manifestation reported to us — the Negative Population Growth movement. This organization wants to make sterilization and abortion mandatory and to deny the new born child his legal personhood until he is one year old. It is a dramatic indication of the development of the contraceptive mentality.

In a more positive vein, the Catholic doctor can and should become an expert on Natural Family Planning, breast feeding and its resultant effects in child spacing. The Catholic doctor can and should be the most logical one to encourage natural childbirth.

If the physician does not feel that he has the time to instruct his patient in Natural Family Planning, he can at least refer couples to organizations which will be glad to help. One such

---

36. Peel, John and Potts, Malcolm, M.D., *Testbook of Contraceptive Practice.* New York: Cambridge University Press, 1969. Peel and Potts note that "breakthrough ovulation" has been observed in 2% to 10% of cycles of women whose cycles have been followed for a considerable time when they were taking oral contraceptives. This raises the question about how the pills achieve their effectiveness in these cases. Some of the combined preparations cause cervical mucus to be hostile to sperm. In addition, however, "it seems likely that the uterine epithelium of a woman taking a serial oral contraceptive is also unsuitable for receiving the fertilized egg even if ovulation and fertilization have taken place," p. 99.

37. In an unpublished address, Dr. Tom Hilgers told his audience that his review of over 400 articles in the medical literature on the operation of the IUD revealed that the evidence was overwhelming that it acted as an abortifacient. "The IUCD — How Does It Work?" Address to the Marriage and Family Life Workshop, St. John's University, Collegeville, Minnesota, June 8, 1972.

Updating of reference 37: Thomas W. Hilgers, M.D. "The Intrauterine Device: Contraceptive or Abortifacient?" *Marriage and Family Newsletter,* Vol. 5, Nos. 1, 2, 3, Jan. - March, 1974. Also in: *Minnesota Medicine,* June, 1974, pp. 493-501.

group is the Couple to Couple League which my wife and I started with the invaluable assistance of Dr. Konald Prem, Professor of Obstetrics and Gynecology at the University of Minnesota.[38]

IV. Conclusion

The theology of dissent has not proven to be intellectually satisfying or convincing and the consequences of contraception are leading former dissenters to accept the traditional doctrine re-affirmed by Paul VI. Such re-thinking has also been stimulated by the overall condition of crisis and decline that has marked Catholic life in the last decade, particularly in the last five years during which the dissenters have been a majority of laity and have also held most of the positions of influence in the American Catholic Church. I submit that such a state of decline would be most difficult to understand if this significant majority were really acting according to the Spirit, but that it is readily understandable if they are in fact acting contrary to the Spirit. Is it not simply a spiritual impossibility to have authentic renewal in the Church if a majority of Catholics are living in "objective" sin and calling it virtue — even if they may escape culpability by reason of ignorance and other factors?

In back of this massive acceptance and practice of contraception has been the premise that this was the only practical way out of a dilemma posed by a combination of sexual urges and the desire for limited family size. Advances in Natural Family Planning have shown that the Author of Nature has provided a way out — one that also develops the same virtues or strengths that are necessary for remaining faithful to the Christian marriage commitment.

The year 1974 has been designated as "population year." It begins the second five year period since *Humanae Vitae*. I have suggested that the simultanaeity of dissent and decline during the first five years post-*Humanae Vitae* has not been

38. Interested parties may write the Couple to Couple League, P.O. Box 11084, Cincinnati, Ohio 45211, for further information.

just coincidental, but that the former has been a significant causal factor in the latter. I submit that the time has come for the theologians and practitioners of dissent to re-direct their considerable energies into support of the sexual tradition of the Church. The next five years can be either a period of restoration and authentic renewal or they can round out what the future will call a decade of decadence.

Catholic physicians can do their patients a great favor by helping them to live within the Church's marital doctrine which allows Natural Family Planning. By doing so they may likewise help to restore health in the Church in our day.